T0196303

Think it.
Do it.
Change it.

Think it.
Do it.
Change it.

How to Dream Big, Act Bold, and Get the Results You Want

ILJA GRZESKOWITZ

With a Foreword by Jeffrey Hayzlett
Primetime Radio & TV Host and Chairman C-Suite Network

GABAL global
English Editions by GABAL Publishing

iUniverse®

iUniverse books may be ordered through booksellers or by contacting:

iUniverse
1663 Liberty Drive
Bloomington, IN 47403
www.iuniverse.com
1-800-Authors (1-800-288-4677)

*Because of the dynamic nature of the Internet, any web addresses or links contained in
this book may have changed since publication and may no longer be valid. The views
expressed in this work are solely those of the author and do not necessarily reflect the views
of the publisher, and the publisher hereby disclaims any responsibility for them.*

*Any people depicted in stock imagery provided by Thinkstock are models,
and such images are being used for illustrative purposes only.
Certain stock imagery © Thinkstock.*

ISBN: 978-1-4917-8719-9 (sc)
ISBN: 978-1-4917-8718-2 (e)

Library of Congress Control Number: 2016900445

Print information available on the last page.

iUniverse rev. date: 1/12/2016

For my daughters, Emma and Elisabeth
You make me happy and proud every single day

Contents

About the Author

Ilja Grzeskowitz (spoken GRAESCH –KO –WITZ) is an award winning keynote speaker, who has given presentations in eight countries on three continents. The change management expert inspires, influences and motivates leaders, entrepreneurs and employees to combine innovative thinking with taking massive action. Some of his clients include BMW, Lufthansa, Telekom and Zalando. He loves to travel all over the world and passionately plays golf. But just in case you're wondering, he is a loving father of two beautiful girls.

The bestselling author of six books studied economics and marketing in Greifswald, Mannheim and Hamburg and held guest lecturing positions at the Berlin School of Law and Economics and the SRH University in Berlin. Before he founded his own company in the year 2009, he was the youngest store manager in Germany's largest retail corporation and was in charge of ten department stores all over the country for Karstadt, Hertie, Wertheim and IKEA.

Today he helps organizations all over the world to create a culture of change. It's no wonder, because this topic has always been the central theme of his life. At the peak of his corporate career, he was regularly fighting at difficult locations, and, together with his teams, he had to find ways to achieve excellent results even under tough circumstances. The experiences he had at that time are a vital part of his speeches, workshops and consultings today. In his programs, he teaches his audiences how to recognize and use the huge opportunities lying in every change. The media called him, "Germany's change expert No.1."

A look into the dictionary: Ilja Grzeskowitz [ˈgræʃkɔvɪts]

1) Keynote Speaker on the topic of change 2) Author of 6 books 3) Changemaker: Special combination of big ideas and taking action 4) Unique brand with a strong personality 5) Change Management Consultant 6) Intensive experience in retail: Former store manager for Karstadt, Hertie, Wertheim und IKEA 7) Walks his talk 8) Awarded with "Audience award for extraordinary speaking skills" and the speaker awards "Best Media 2013" und "Best Performer 2014" 9) Likes golf, traveling around the world und dining out 10) Loves his family 11) Questions the status quo since 1975

Contact

www.grzeskowitz.com
www.facebook.com/igrzeskowitz
www.twitter.com/igrzeskowitz

Foreword by Jeffrey Hayzlett

When Ilja asked me to write the foreword to this book, I jumped at the chance because I knew *Think it. Do it. Change it.* would align with my personal mantra to think big and act bigger. In the book, Ilja details his motivations and advice for changing your business and life. It will never be the perfect time to pursue your dreams, so stop making excuses and just do it! You might fail the first time and the second time, but, for the most part, no one is going to die. You need to challenge yourself in order to achieve your goals and Ilja will arm you with the skills you need to overcome those challenges. He is declaring war on the "wait and see" society and I'm joining him in that battle.

After speaking with Ilja about his inspiration for the book and then reading *Think it. Do it. Change it.,* I was reminded of a story from my past. I had been Chief Marketing Officer (CMO) at a Fortune 100 company for several years when I left to build my personal brand as a speaker, strategic business consultant, and media personality. I had spent my years as a CMO fighting against deep-seeded "big company" limitations and was looking forward to getting back to the wide-eyed optimism, control, intimacy, and seemingly endless possibilities of being an entrepreneur. I wanted to build a dynamic, nimble business with just a small team that I could guide anywhere I wanted to go.

The first place I set out to build my brand was online. I challenged my team to figure out a way to boost my social presence with 25,000 fans on Twitter and Facebook. I wanted a plan that would allow me to do this and do it fast. The team put together a strong plan with one gaping flaw; it was a plan to get me 15,000 fans.

"Why?" I asked.

"Our budget."

"But I never gave you a budget! I just asked you to tell me what it would take to get where we needed to go."

My response was met with silence from the team. When I made this request, I understood there would be challenges we would need to overcome but I was prepared to tackle them. The team was setting a self-imposed limitation without considering a solution. They weren't thinking big or acting bigger. Over the last few years, I have learned to think big and act bigger in everything I do. I tie visions to actions and push past the limitations. I'm bold, fearless, and even and occasionally a little pigheaded. I've learned to be relentless in all I do, especially trusting in who I am—*because I can.*

As a Fortune 100 CMO, I would sit in board meetings with the rest of the c-level executives and think, *They must know something I don't know or they must be smarter than me.* What I didn't realize at the time was they weren't. They were more confident in their skillset and they trusted their gut instinct. Since this realization, I have always gone with my gut instinct. So I challenge you to trust your gut and just do it—after reading Ilja's book, of course.

Jeffrey Hayzlett, Primetime Radio & TV Host, Bestselling Author and Sometime Cowboy

Introduction: What if...?

"But no one, no nobody can give you the power to rise over love. Over hate. Through this iron sky that's fast becoming our mind. Over fear and into freedom. You've just got to hold on."
                                                                    - Paolo Nutini, Iron Sky

It was an ordinary Tuesday in the fall of 1994, and, even though nothing exceptional was happening in the world that day, I will probably never forget it. Because in one single instant, my own world was turned upside down. At the time, I was completing my eighteen months of civil service at an integrated facility at the university hospital of my hometown, Lübeck. In addition to children with learning and developmental difficulties, we also took care of patients on various wards, to make their everyday hospital life a little less boring. One of the children had earned a really special place in my heart. Tommy was a nine-year-old boy who was in the pediatric cancer ward due to a brain tumor. He had already gone through multiple surgeries and had no hair left on his head. Instead, two large scars crossed his bald skull—external tracks that showed the doctors' desperate fight against this vicious disease. But the cancer had already spread so far that it was impossible for Tommy to win the fight. One thing was remarkable though. Despite the shocking diagnosis, this brave boy was the happiest kid in our entire institution. With an infectious passion, he was carving little wooden figures at the workbench, played puzzles for hours or practiced songs by Cat Stevens on the guitar. And when he became too exhausted to continue, he loved it when I read him one of the adventures of Asterix and Obelix.

Tommy's overwhelming lust for life fascinated me. He had every possible reason in the world to be depressed, but he simply wasn't. Instead, he laughed a lot, was always in a good mood and passed his courage on to the other children. But at the same time, his physical condition started to get worse rapidly, and there were days when I didn't see Tommy at all. But on that special Tuesday, he was sitting on my lap again and we read *Asterix in Spain* together. Everything seemed like it always was, but when we got to his favorite part (for insiders: When little Pepe holds his breath because he does not want to eat fish), Tommy casually said these words that I will never forget: "Ilja, I know I am going to die soon. But I'm not afraid, because I know God is watching over me. By the way, I wanted to tell you that I like it when we're reading together. The nurses never feel like doing it. As a thank you, I will carve you a talisman tomorrow." Even though I had a hard time fighting back the tears in that moment, I forced myself not to let it show. Instead, I just said, "Cool, I look forward to it." Then I continued reading until we parted ways with our usual high-five shortly after. I never did get my talisman, because Tommy died two days later.

Being only nineteen years old at that time, it took me quite a while to digest what had happened on that day; but on an intuitive, deeper level, I knew that, even under these tragic circumstances, this brave little boy had given me something very special. I learned more about motivation from that encounter than from all the books, seminars and talks over the many years that have followed since. With his life-affirming attitude, he opened my eyes and showed me what a huge difference a single human being can make, even if all the odds seem to be against him. He taught me that a little boy can be a role model, showing us how to set the world on fire and effect real change. Because he knew he didn't have much time left, he enjoyed every single moment to the fullest and lived it with an intensity that was contagious to every child and adult around him.

And even though it still breaks my heart that Tommy died far too early, I am really grateful that he taught me an important lesson. Back then, in a kind of naive ritual, I swore to myself I'd make the most of every single moment of my life. I decided to become successful, to start a career and to experience all the things that Tommy had been denied. At that time I had no idea how I would get there, but looking back I know that this was one of the major turning points of my life. To this day, I haven't stopped drawing from that lesson. Whenever I'm about to get upset about some petty thing, I remind myself of how grateful every one of us should be that we are healthy and alive, and that we have another day's chance to leave the world a little better than we found it.

At this point, I would like to extend a warm welcome to all of my readers. Knowing that time is your scarcest resource, I very much appreciate your trust and confidence in me. I have long considered whether it would be a good idea to begin a book about motivation and change with a story about death. After all, nothing is more important to me than supporting you on your personal journey with life-affirming, inspirational and solution-oriented ideas. More than once I pushed the memories of Tommy back into my virtual drawer and experimented with different beginnings. But, as it often is with big ideas, they keep coming back and demand to be put into practice. And isn't it exactly the realization that life is finite that often makes us reconsider our motivations and radically change course?

How many people do you know who are so afraid of necessary changes that they continue to live by the expectations of others rather than follow through on their own ideas about how to live their life? How many people do you know who take refuge in the illusion of safety, instead of living every single day with joy and passion? Who are waiting for the perfect moment instead of taking action, until one day they realize with a sense of nostalgia that their dreams have silently died. Whose only motivation is the promise of their favorite TV show in the evening. And very often, it takes a crisis, a blow of fate, or an encounter with death, for that matter, to cause them to regret all the things they haven't done, known or experienced. The longer I thought about it the more I realized that this book could have no better beginning than a story focusing on the fact that each of us will eventually die and a happy life cannot be taken for granted.

> Always remember that life is finite. So start making every day count.

Right at the beginning, I'd like to remind you of one thing. You should never forget that our time on this planet is limited and may end earlier than we expect.

Therefore, we should enjoy it as much as possible and make the most of each and every area of life. We should work, love, and live every single second as if nothing more important existed in the world. But what do most people do? They keep their dreams and intentions locked in a drawer, have a job they don't like and live in relationships that do not make them happy. Someday, of course, they are planning to do something about it. But for the time being, it simply isn't possible, because their full schedules leave them with no choice. And so they keep on waiting for the right moment—days, weeks, months, or even years. But hoping for a vague *someday* is often deceptive, as it eventually turns into a *never*.

And one day, when they look back, they suddenly regret that they haven't taken more risks, enjoyed the beautiful things in life and had the courage to live their dreams. With a deep sense of sadness, they realize how many opportunities they have not pursued, how many fears they have not overcome and how many goals they have not achieved. Isn't it true that we often only value what we are about to lose? I still remember how it felt when I had to wear a plaster around my right arm because of a broken wrist. No big deal, one would say; however, the simplest daily routines suddenly became a challenge. When I finally got rid of the plaster I felt more grateful than ever for being able to eat in a normal way, tie my shoes, and drive my car. As Jim Rohn aptly put it, "There are two types of pain you will go through in life, the pain of discipline and the pain of regret," to which I'd like to add that you can only avoid one of them at a time. It's a choice we have to make every day.

Don't you think that we are taking far too many opportunities for granted? Examples include our jobs, the people in our lives and, most importantly, our health. We should be grateful for everything that is given to us and then make a conscious decision to never settle for the status quo, but to strive for extraordinary results in every single area of our life. We should commit to not letting our dreams die, instead doing everything to make them real—not in some distant future, but today. Start doing things that wake you up in the middle of the night craving for adventure even if they come with risks. Start your own business, build a career, meet your dream partner, travel around the world, engage in a good cause, write a book, tell your children how much you love them, change your diet, experience unforgettable sunsets, and do as much as possible of what fills your heart with joy. As an old proverb says, "The best time to plant a tree is twenty years ago, the second best is now." The same is true for your intentions and dreams. If you take the first step today, in twelve months' time you will be very glad you did.

> Start living your dreams today. The best time for a change is now.

Have the guts to take charge of your life. A ship lying in the harbor is safe; however, it has been built to sail through stormy seas. The same is true for your inner passion. You have been born into this world to make a difference. Of course, you could avoid all possible risks, stay in the alleged safe harbor and manage the status quo for the rest of your life, occasionally throwing a longing glance at the horizon. But you might as well hoist the anchor, set sail, and embark on a future in which you live your dreams to the fullest. Of course, there is always the risk of shipwreck, but what might look like a failure is actually a great opportunity to grow. Far more agonizing is the feeling you experience when you have waited until it is eventually too late. The burden of discipline weighs ounces. The burden of regret weighs a ton.

The more often we bring this fact to our attention, the fuller a life we can live, using every single day to become the best possible version of ourselves. To do that, you need to sit in the driver's seat, no matter where the journey of your life has taken you so far. Free yourself from titles, money and other people's permission and find your own motivation for change. Become a Changemaker, a term I should define right now as I'm going to use it quite often in this book. In my eyes, a Changemaker is a person who views the small and big changes in life as great opportunities, and who combines this can-do attitude with a strong ability to take massive action. Changemakers actively seek out chances and possibilities to design their own futures rather than just managing the status quo. They let their actions speak louder than their words. When the chips are down, they stand their ground, being role models for their people, customers, and colleagues. In a nutshell, a Changemaker is a person who does not leave their career, relationships and overall quality of life to chance but is instead committed to living every single second to the very fullest.

> Changemakers don't need titles, money or permission to take action.

Well, have you been able to identify with some of these suggestions? Is there work to be done here or there? To help you determine how much of a Changemaker you already are, I'd like to invite you to perform a short thought experiment. Imagine yourself at the end of your days sitting as an old and (hopefully) wise person in a comfortable rocking chair on your veranda. Enjoying the skin-warming evening sun, you let the years of your life pass before your mind's eye. Looking back at your professional career, your family life and the development of your potential, would you be grateful and proud because you lived a fulfilled life full of magic moments, or would your thoughts be rather sad, because of all the goals you have never achieved, all the risks you have never taken and all the dreams you have never lived?

In this hypothetical flashback, have you actively changed the world and lived your ideas, or have you passively waited, surrendered to the circumstances, other people's decisions and external conditions? Have you been a game changer or a manager of the status quo? Whatever your answer to this fictitious thought is, I'd like to encourage you to take the road of the Changemaker by assuming responsibility for your own life and being a role model to others. I'd like to inspire you to make the very best of your career, your relationships and your general satisfaction; to unleash your full potential and make a difference. If you are already on a good track, I'd like to challenge you to up the ante and take the next step from good to great. And if you sometimes get the feeling that this can't have been everything, it would mean the world to me if you would choose this book to be your personal wake-up call.

Whatever your starting point looks like, today is the best moment to set the course for a future in which you have a firm grip on the reins, decide both direction and speed, and enjoy the roller coaster ride we call life. In which you change actively, become a role model for others and unhinge the world by your feats. In which you take care of your actions and leave your mark in the world. At this point you may object with, "Well, Ilja, I'm just an everyday person. There isn't much I can change." My answer is this: "You don't even know what you are capable of." Why shouldn't you be able to do what so many have succeeded in doing before? The most important thing is that you start from where you are now, focusing on your inner motivation. And by doing so, sometimes things will happen that you couldn't even have imagined in your wildest dreams. When your inner fire starts to burn, it can easily develop into an inferno. Soon, you are going to realize that the people in your environment change as well. I'd even say the more you try to make a difference on a small scale rather than change the world at large, the more likely you are to leave a really big mark.

I can hear your next objection. "Only people who are already successful can make a real impact. Don't you need a title, money and certain connections to bring about changes?" My clear and unequivocal answer is, "No, on the contrary." Did Steve Jobs and his friends need a title to create the Apple empire in a garage in Los Altos? Did Martin Luther King Jr. need money to share his dream with millions of people? Did Steve Bezos need other people's permission to launch the Internet empire Amazon? These are all examples showing the possible impact of starting small and having the guts to use your potential to become the best version of yourself.

And with that we have reached the red thread, the central theme of this book. You don't need a title, money or permission to live a successful life. You don't need a title to lead as a role model and inspire the people around you. You don't need money to increase your sales, be passionate about your work and go the extra mile for your customers. You don't need anybody's permission to make bold decisions and exceed others' expectations. All of this happens by itself as you overcome the fear of change and start developing big ideas, making clear decisions and acting with confidence. Let the title of this book become your daily mantra: "*Think it. Do it. Change it.*"

No matter what kind of job you have today, here is a big idea for you. A job is an ordinary job only as long as you choose it to be ordinary. It doesn't matter whether you are an apprentice, employee, public official, manager or the CEO of your company, any activity in this world is a unique opportunity to use your full potential and leave your mark on your environment. So please let go of the idea that your personal success depends on external conditions. Whatever you need to initiate, be it small or large changes in your life, is already in you. Your huge potential is waiting for you to tap into and develop it.

> Become the best possible version of yourself. You will be a role model for the people around you.

But if this is so simple, why do so few people have the guts to unhinge the world? Because, while things may seem clear in theory, the practical execution is quite a different story. In my daily work as a keynote speaker and change coach, it frequently occurs to me how much our society has become a collection of whiners, grumblers and negative people. Nobody seems to be happy anymore. Nobody is aware of the great opportunities these exciting times provide. Everybody seems to expect that it's up to other people to change so that they can stay as they are. But when everybody waits for somebody then nobody will ever do anything and nothing will change at all. Just waiting for your boss, your co-workers or your spouse to make the right decisions for you is a sure route to mediocrity, and, thus, to unhappiness. Don't let that happen. Decide to make a difference right now.

Take the lead and have the courage to leave the stamp of your personality on life. Act on your values and ideas. Make your own decisions. Don't let your dreams die silently, but scream to the world how much you love your life. If you consequently apply this philosophy, your daily life will be much more colorful, your business more successful, your career more rewarding and your general well-being more intense. Sounds quite good, doesn't it? But be assured that it's not that easy. It is much easier to rely on others, to hide in the crowd and become a conformist sheep in the herd. Taking responsibility as a leader is the hard, stony and risky path. Because when you take charge of your own motivation that immediately puts you in the pioneer's role. You will walk along paths no one has ever walked before. You will be making decisions that could be right or wrong. You will be making mistakes. Many mistakes. Big mistakes. But you will also learn from these mistakes and grow as a person. And that is the crucial point. Only if you feel a deep and meaningful motivation yourself are you able to motivate others. Only if you become a better human being are you able to become a better entrepreneur, supervisor, or colleague. Only if you grow as a person can your professional results grow as well.

It is my daily job to help entrepreneurs, executives, and managers implement this growth process in the best possible manner. Dear reader, I'd like to encourage you to no longer rely on external factors and other people to motivate you, but to actively initiate the necessary changes in your company, your family and the various situations of everyday life. Always remember, if you don't do it nobody will. Therefore, I would be very honored if you would use this book as your faithful companion and constant source of inspiration.

It is not my intention to tell you how to live your life. It took me thirty years, after all, to have the courage to free myself from titles, money, and other people's permission and take charge of my own life. Believe me, to get to this point I had to fight the same demons as everybody else. I, too, had doubts and fears. And more than once I was on the verge of resignation. Even today, for every mountain to be conquered there is a valley that must be crossed first. And, nevertheless, again and again, I hear the same objections, "Well, Ilja, it may be easy for you, but my situation is much more complicated. I would never be able to do what you did." Let me therefore make two things clear. First, you shouldn't compare yourself either to me or to anybody else, as people are simply too different.

You mustn't necessarily throw away your successful job and start again from scratch, as I did. Find your own way and let your values and visions guide you, whether as an entrepreneur, executive, or manager. But even if you are an employee, a housewife or a student you can no

> Change actively. Don't wait for others to give you permission.

less live the life of a Changemaker, lead as a role model, and motivate others. My second point is even more important. I don't have any exceptional talents or extraordinary capabilities. It's more like the famous German TV host Thomas Gottschalk once said, "There is nothing I'm really good at, except talking and entertaining people." When I consider my own abilities, there are many things I'm all but good at. But I have reached a point in my personal development where that doesn't frustrate me anymore. Instead, I rather focus on what I am really good at, and that is talking, writing and creating a culture of change. Let me be really clear; I'm neither unique nor a guru who has discovered the one and only path to the truth. I am just a normal guy who has made the same mistakes, struggled with the same problems and had to fight the same demons as you did.

I, too, have experienced situations where I was under remote control, relying on others to make sure that I was motivated to do my work; where I refused to do anything on my own initiative, convinced that, without a title, money or permission, nothing could be achieved in the first place. I, too, kept my dreams locked in a drawer, believing that the right moment was yet to come. However, by making the principles of this book my guiding philosophy, I was able to free myself from this passive way of living. It wasn't easy, but eventually I was bold enough. I chose to take the hard, stony and risky road. On my journey, I made lots of mistakes, but I also learned fast and grew with the challenges. And the more I evolved on the inside, the more the success became visible on the outside.

But I never would have made it without the help of so many wonderful people. Since I'll never forget that, it has become my mission to spread the ideas from my experiences in keynote speeches, seminars and, most importantly, books. Let me share with you a fundamental belief. I am deeply convinced that each of us has a mission, a purpose, or a vocation in life. You, too, were born with a unique personality. You have very special talents and capabilities to discover and develop in the course of your life. But that is only possible if you decide to take responsibility, become a critical thinker and lead by example. To do that it is necessary to leave the comfort zone of uncommittedness and to have the guts to become the best version of yourself; to start actively designing your life and from there to kick off a huge wave of change.

If you are prepared to embark on this journey, I'm looking forward to being your companion. To help you even more, I'd like to conduct a little experiment. This is a very personal book that grants you quite a view of my inner world. To be able to share my emotions on different levels with you, each chapter begins with a song that has inspired my writing. The book will thus be accompanied by a sound track, and I hope that the combination of music, lyrics and my ideas will have the same special impact on you that it had on me.[1]

And there's more. To give you the best support I possibly can, I founded a private Facebook group, which is only open to readers of this book. There, you not only have the opportunity to get tips and tricks from me personally, but also to share your ideas, thoughts and challenges with people from all over the world. The general intention is a huge mastermind group, which only has one purpose: To support you on

> Leave your mark on the world. Ignite your inner motivation and let the spark jump over.

your individual journey. Here is the link to the group; it would mean the world to me if you would join the movement: https://www.facebook.com/groups/MachEsEinfach

And now take out your dreams from the drawer and start living a life characterized by possibilities rather than limitations. From today onwards,

---

[1] You'll find the link to the Spotify Playlist at the end of the book in the "Bibliography" section

try to be a better boss, employee or spouse than you were yesterday. Together, let us cross deep valleys and climb big mountains. Let us replace indifference and mediocrity with commitment and awesomeness. Don't wait for others to tell you what to do, but take responsibility yourself. Most of all, don't wait to make these decisions until someone else gives you permission. It all depends on you. Choose to become the best version of yourself and leave your mark on the world. Ignite the fire of your inner motivation and let the spark jump over. Let us change the world together—on a small scale or even on a big one. In this book, I'll gladly take the lead. It would be a great honor to have you on my team. Are you in?

Sincerely yours,
Ilja Grzeskowitz
Berlin – Miami Beach – Bangkok, Spring 2015

Stop Waiting -
Why the Perfect Moment Will Never Come

"And I think it's gonna be a long, long, time, 'til touchdown brings me 'round again to find, I'm not the man they think I am at home. Ah, no no no, I'm a rocket man."

- Elton John, Rocket Man

It's Monday, June 16th, 2014. I am sitting at the Panke, a small river north of Berlin, and am enjoying my day. There is not a cloud in the sky and the temperature has already reached seventy-seven degrees at eleven o'clock in the morning. Since I have been traveling almost nonstop for speeches lately, I am using my first free day in weeks to relax a little. And as I am letting the mental images of the past experiences pass by, my eyes catch a piece of wood that is floating with the current of the water. This observation is fascinating me. Every movement is more or less random and the course is determined by outside influences. From time to time, this piece of wood gets caught on a rock or a plant, until it disappears from my view, caught by a faster rapid.

And I don't remember exactly what it was, but in that moment I had to think about how many people live their life according to this pattern. You float around more or less randomly, without having a clear goal or a specific vision. You'd rather wait and adjust, instead of actively creating your future. This pattern of leading a passive life has grave consequences. Everyone relies on someone else to take responsibility. Nobody is brave enough to make decisions anymore. Nobody wants to make mistakes. Course, direction and speed of your own life are subject to a fatal arbitrariness, and, at some point, you come to terms with this discontent that is undoubtedly going to occur.

You would rather manage the status quo than take destiny into your own two hands and initiate the necessary changes yourself.

I want to give you a typical example. I was recently leading a workshop with managers of a middle-management level who were responsible for a branch of a big company, with revenues in the double digits of millions. I know many executives who would have given their left eye for a job like this. But the persons acting thought of their own situation as a huge burden. Had there not been a definition of standstill, you could have found it there, live and in full color. The cause for this was, mostly, that the former branch manager died a few years ago, and he had made all decisions cordially, but ultimately, patriarchally. Everyone involved got comfortable with the situation and everything worked more or less smoothly.

But even though the responsibilities were theoretically distributed across several shoulders, after the death of the former boss, a treacherous void arose. The outcome was fatal. Projects were left behind, important customers were lost and, all in all, an atmosphere of uncertainty reigned, which paralyzed all employees. And the reaction of the gathered managment team made it clear to me, once again, how high the need is for people who lead by example and with a high intrinsic motivation. Because when I asked, "Who was responsible for the big and small changes in the company in the past few months?" the question was naturally answered by one of the present managers with, "Well, nobody. We didn't have anyone who could have made these decisions!"

> Don't settle for a passive lifestyle, but take destiny in your own hands.

Are you Still Hesitating or Are you Taking Action?

How about you, my dear readers, how many times have you found yourself in a situation where you thought, *Somebody definitely needs to do something with this*? How many times would you have liked to have changed something but relied on someone else taking care of it? How many times were you dissatisfied with a certain area in your life, but you hesitated for so long that everything remained how it's always been in the end? Trust me, I know this behavior all too well from my own past. I truly was an expert in passing off responsibilities, and hoping that others would make the right decisions for me. But one day I realized where this attitude had led me, namely a life characterized by external direction and discontent. And by no means was it easy for me to free myself from this behavior pattern and take full responsibility for all my ideas, decisions and actions.

Because I know what I am talking about, this book is a matter that's very dear to my heart. My current profession as a keynote speaker and change consultant gives me the privilege of working with various types of people. And aside from social, economical and hierarchical status, there is one thing I observe almost on a daily basis. With a fatalistic peace of mind, the majority relies on others to show them the way and to make the necessary decisions for them—all because of the widely publicized misbelief that you need a title, money or permission to successfully initiate change. But this way of thinking has grave consequences, because, slowly, you forget how to take responsibility, to change actively and use your own potential to it's fullest. It always breaks my heart when I meet people who possess unique talents, amazing abilities and that are blessed with an admirable creativity, and they just let these gifts waste away.

And just in case you should think that there are only a select few who are privileged enough to have these kind of gifts, then I'd like to share one of my deepest beliefs with you. Inside every single person, a huge potential lies dormant that is just waiting to be brought to the surface and be used. And it doesn't matter what profession you are currently in, what title you have, or which starting point you are beginning from. It also does not matter

> Living an active life means to take personal responsibility, to change actively and to use your full potential.

if you are a successful business owner, or a housewife and mother. The one and only thing that matters is whether you are ready to continue evolving. The world is waiting to be moved, namely by you. "But Ilja," you might object, "how can I change my business, my surroundings or even the world? I can't even find the time to organize my everyday life properly. Besides, I don't have any connections, or enough power or money."

Believe me; I can understand these objections because I hear them nearly every single day. But I decided a long time ago not to accept these excuses any longer. Because even if you have been told on a regular basis that those people who move the world have extraordinary skills at their disposal, this could not be further from the truth. Quite the contrary, it's always people like you who steadily put the biggest dents in the universe. It's people like you who make a difference with their ideas and innovations. It's people like you who make the world a better place every day through their decisions and actions. So start doing it and stop waiting for your boss, your colleagues, or your social environment to give you permission. All that you need to awaken your personal motivation to change you already carry inside of you. You doubt this statement? Then let us look at the following factors together, that nobody but you can influence.

Ten things that you can influence at any time, even under difficult conditions

1. You can go through life with a positive attitude each day.
2. You can be a role model to other people every day through your thoughts, decisions and actions.
3. You can complete your work with passion, ambition and motivation each day.
4. You can work on your own personal development every day.
5. You can use every day to dream big and make bold choices.
6. You can make other people happy every day.
7. You can make sure your colleagues, customers and co-workers follow your lead through high standards and expectations.
8. You can give everything, every single day, to be better than you were yesterday.
9. You can take another step on the way to greatness every day.
10. You can use your talents, your abilities and your experiences every day to become a better version of yourself.

Do you see what I mean? You don't need a title, money or permission from others for any of these things. It's all up to you. And nobody expects you to save the entire world right away (I think this is best left to Eric Clapton). No, you should start with yourself, at your workplace, in your family and your environment. One of my favorites quotes is from Mother Teresa, who once said "If each of us would only clean their own doorstep, the world would be clean." Right she is, this remarkable lady. Change always begins on the inside and then comes to the light through our actions.

If you have internalized this basic rule, a whole new world is going to open up in front of you. Outside circumstances, external events or other people are not the starting point of changes in your life. If you want to be, do or have something different, the origin always lies within yourself. You have to be the spark that ignites the big fire of change. And that's exactly why this book has the title *Think it. Do it. Change it.* No matter what it is that you want to change, don't wait for others, but always lead by example because your personal development and your outside results are inseparably interlocked. They follow a clear order, which, again, I will summarize for you in ten aspects.

Ten external successes that originate on the inside

1. If you grow as a person, your quality of life will also grow.
2. If you help yourself, you can also help others.
3. If you care for yourself, you can also care for others.
4. If you are motivated, you can motivate others as well.
5. If you become the best version of yourself, you can also develop the potential of others.
6. If you are inspired, you can also inspire others.
7. If you focus on chances and opportunities, your environment can also become more positive.
8. If you appreciate yourself, you will also appreciate the people around you.
9. If you build yourself up, you can build up a successful business as well.
10. If you change yourself, you can also change the world.

There are so many wonderful gifts just lying dormant inside of you, just waiting to be exalted and utilized. If you want to, you can start immediately. All you need for this is a decision, the unconditional commitment to immediately take responsibility for your results, your career and your life. And before you know it, you set off a giant domino effect that will transfer over to your co-workers, colleagues and customers. This will happen as soon as you stop waiting and boldly move forward instead, acting as a leader for your co-workers, customers and colleagues on the way. When you don't expect anything from others that you wouldn't be willing to do yourself; when you let your actions speak louder than your words; when you change yourself first—then watch how everything around you starts to change as well.

> Change always starts on the inside. Through our actions it becomes visible on the outside.

If You Don't Change, You Will Get Changed

In my book, *Die Veränderungs-Formel: Aus Problemen Chancen machen* (*The Change Formula: Turning Problems into Chances*), I put forward the theory that the successful handling of the ever-accelerating change is going to be the most important key competence of the future. Since then, a few months have passed and a look at a newspaper of your choice (or the online version, if you prefer that medium) is enough to see how much my statement has hit the mark. Society is changing, the world is spinning faster and permanent change has become a daily companion. The rules have changed and values have shifted. What was the standard yesterday can already be outdated today.

In my job as a keynote speaker and change consultant, I work in the most diverse companies and different industries. And there is one question that I get asked over and over again: "Ilja, the changes won't stop, and we've already restructured a hundred times, when is it going to get back to normal again?" To that, I usually give the following answer, "But what if this is it? What if the constant change has long become the new normal? The question today is not *if* you have been affected by change, but how well are you prepared for it, and how do you deal with it?"

And this is where it gets interesting. Instead of making the necessary changes, many people have specialized in waiting for the perfect moment. By doing so, they miss out on taking their career to the next level, improving the atmosphere at their workplace or making a long-standing dream become reality. The companies also haven't adjusted to the changed conditions yet. In some cases, I even get the impression that some organizations have mentally stopped in their tracks over thirty years ago. In practice, these crusty structures are often reflected through hierarchical thinking, a strict top-down leadership, and, because of this, an inevitably large amount of bureaucracy. The thinking is simple. The longer and more exotic the title listed on the manager's business card, the more power he has, as a general rule. But this mentality leads to decision paths being dragged out, responsibilities being delegated from the bottom up, and changes taking a very long time, or never happening at all.

In day-to-day business, this has huge consequences. If the executive floor doesn't make any decisions, nothing happens at all. The result? Slowly but surely, a culture of apathy starts developing, in which you lean back, wait it out and rely on someone else fixing things for you. And before you now it, you find yourself in a dilemma. While the belief manifests itself that changes without an official instruction are impossible, you're giving away your personal responsibility step by step. You forget that you have the ability to make your own decisions, question strategic developments and change yourself. You'd rather whine (usually at a very high level) about the demanding customers, the lazy colleagues or external circumstances than take the necessary steps to initiate changes yourself.

That this can be different is something I recently became very aware of, when I flew back to Berlin after a business meeting in Frankfurt. If you are a more or less frequent flyer yourself, you will know that you can sometimes get really lucky with the person sitting next to you. Emphasis on *sometimes*. On that particular day, I wanted to get some work done, so directly after boarding I opened my MacBook Air,

> Say goodbye to the growing culture of apathy and start making your own decisions.

and I was hoping to write a few more pages for my new book during the flight. It was a clear signal for the outside world: I want to be left alone. But the person sitting next to me did not pay any mind, because he started talking to me before the plane even took off. "So, are you flying to Berlin, too?" I really wanted to reply, "Nope, I'm getting off over Hannover!" But the ice was broken and we talked about his current job situation for almost the entire flight. He was a manager in a company that was involved in an intensive change process. And his attitude really did impress me because he said, "You know, Mr. Grzeskowitz, our situation definitely isn't easy, but I think about it like this. Even if the circumstances are tough, there are things that I can control and there are things I can't control. And I've decided to exclusively focus on the first category."

Pretty impressive, right? Could you say the same thing about yourself if I were to ask you what you focus on normally? For that matter, the choice of focus is generally quite obvious. You can't control what happens around you anyway. You can't control the changing economy, what the competition is doing or how your spouse is acting. Just view these external circumstances as a given. But you can control how you react to them at any time. And all of your energy should be used exactly for this—for the things that you *can* change. This attitude shift alone gives you a great deal of power, which you should consciously apply as often as you can.

Here's a practical example. A few years ago, I spent my vacation in Huntington Beach. The city is located south of LA and is mostly known for two things. Soccer legend Jürgen Klinsmann lives there and the beach is considered the surf mecca of the USA. And the local surfers have a great slogan, "You can't stop the waves, but you can learn how to ride them."

And this is exactly the mentality I am talking about. No matter how challenging the situation might seem, you always have a choice. Whether you become part of the problem or start focusing on a possible solution. Whether you feel like a victim of external circumstances or take responsibility. Whether you change actively or passively wait to see what happens around you. But what do most people do? They wait and wait and wait and only then start acting, when the outside circumstances force them to do so. And, suddenly, change has arrived, whether you like it or not. So, cross your heart, have you ever been in a situation where you thought, *I wish I had taken action sooner?*

And though I could have done without it, I know the feeling all too well. Last year, two homes in our neighborhood were broken into. So my wife said to me, "We definitely need an alarm system."

I answered, "No, if somebody wants to break in, an alarm system won't stop them."

She said, "Yes, we do need one."

I countered, "No, we don't."

She said, "Yes."

I said, "No." You know this game of relationship ping-pong, don't you? And it probably would have gone on forever if I didn't know the big secret of a good and lasting relationship. The man always has to have the last two words in a disagreement: "Yes, dear."

So, two weeks later, an alarm system was installed. Since that day we no longer have a lock, and instead of keys we are using programmable plastic chips. The system is controlled by a computer unit, which is located in my office. It is a true all-around talent. It programs the motion sensors, activates the system, deactivates it again, and even calls you on your cell phone if an alarm is triggered. Pretty complicated. The technician even asked, after the installation, "Do you want me to explain how to operate it?"

Well, maybe you know that there are four classic phases of change: Suppression. Resistance. Acceptance. Commitment. And at that moment I found myself right in the middle of phase two. Heavy resistance. That's why I answered, "No, not necessary." Because it wasn't me who wanted to install that system in the first place and, secondly, how hard can it be? After making this bold statement, I set off a false alarm with

> Always shift your focus on to the things you can control. Don't get distracted.

my new chip multiple times in the next three days. And every time my wife had to disarm the system.

Visibly irritated, she said, "Listen, Ilja, I'm getting annoyed. You're not even trying. And it's really not that hard. If the red light flashes, that means the system is armed. Green means it's not. And if the alarm goes off, all you have to do is type in your four-digit pin to disarm it. Did you memorize it?"

Of course I had not. Nevertheless, I again said, "Yes, dear."

But if you don't actively change, you will get changed at some point. And I don't know if it was by chance or fate, but a few days later my wife took the kids to her father's birthday celebration over the weekend. I didn't join them because I had a keynote speech in Switzerland that day and returned home very late. After a stressful journey back to Berlin, I was looking forward to my comfortable bed and probably would have slept for twelve uninterrupted hours—if I hadn't been woken up by a suspicious beep at four am. And I knew it right away; it was the stupid alarm system.

So I went to see what was going on. Because it was pitch black in the whole house, I flipped the light switch in the hallway. Nothing happened. I went back into the bedroom and tried the switch there. Again nothing. Not one light switch was working in the entire house. In my desperation, I opened the flashlight app on my iPhone and went to the fuse box. Everything was fine. All the fuses were in their place. Slowly, I started feeling a bit uneasy. I looked outside. Not one streetlight was on. No lights in any of the windows. The entire street was dark. The uneasy feeling got stronger. And the alarm system was still beeping. With my iPhone flashlight, I went to the computer unit in my office and started pressing buttons randomly. And I must have hit the right ones, because, suddenly, it was quiet. I was just about to pat myself on the back when I heard a distorted voice coming out of the unit, "The alarm system has been activated." And three seconds later I triggered the alarm through one of the motion sensors.

Now please imagine a deafeningly loud alarm sound on top of total darkness. I was just about to panic when my iPhone started ringing. I answered and listened to a recorded message, "An alarm was triggered. To confirm, please press nine." But I didn't have time because I had to turn the alarm off. So back to the terminal. And what did it say on the display in big, bright letters? "Please enter your four-digit pin number." And right then, in that moment, I had the deciding thought, *Why did I not take action sooner?* But now it was too late. So back to concentrating. What was the pin? I knew it had to do with a birthday. I entered four numbers: 3175. Nothing. 7513. Nothing again. I tried all variations. Nothing. The alarm just would not stop.

What was I to do? Even though I was sufficiently embarrassed, I grabbed my iPhone and dialed my wife's cell number. After what felt like an eternity, the call was answered. By her voicemail. Now I had only one other option. At four-thirty in the morning, I called my in-laws' home number. And a minute and a heavy lecture later, I knew my pin again. I entered the four numbers, and everything was silent once again. I'd had a lucky escape.

How do you deal with change, dear readers? Are you actively changing, or do you prefer to wait for the perfect moment and hope that you'll get a lucky break? Today, I am able to laugh about this story, but in that moment I learned something very important. Always be prepared and focus on chances and opportunities. Because if you don't actively change, you will get changed at some point. And this is why I want to invite you to leave the times of passively waiting behind you, once and for all. Set the pin code for your life yourself. Be one step ahead of the changes. And this starts with the decision to take responsibility, even though this might not be the easy way. Make the conscious decision to look in the mirror and say, "No matter where

I am today, no matter how satisfied or dissatisfied I am with my results, it was always me. Nobody else. And if I don't like it, only I can change it."

When the audiences during my speeches hear this sentence for the first time, I normally receive approving nods. But please don't let yourself be deceived. Even though the philosophy behind it is easy to understand in theory, the practical application is an entirely separate matter. Many people really try hard and wish nothing more than to break free from the chains of dependency. They dream of creating their own workplace, their personal environment, and their future

> If you don't change actively, you will get changed.

themselves. But often all that's missing is the belief that such a mentality is suitable for everyday life, because early in our childhood we are already being convinced of the concept that changes are always something that other people initiate.

Already in school, our children are taught to adapt as soon as possible. In neat rows, they sit behind desks, growing up with lesson plans that haven't been updated in years and learn the hard way that there is no room for individuality, creativity and personal responsibility in the classroom. And before you know it, this way of learning is hammered deep into our minds and we rely on others to make the right decisions for us—first our teachers then our bosses and, in the end, the all-caring nanny state. Official titles, power and hierarchical positions have become false gods that we look up to and rely upon. We sit in our protected bubble, become a good sheep in the middle of the herd and eventually function according to the demands, expectations and rules of others.

But if everyone waits for *someone else* to take care of things, a standstill is imminent. The time has come to break out of this vicious cycle and set an example. Stop waiting for others and start changing actively. Create your own career, your own business and your own world with your personality. And just to address this clearly, of course it is no obstacle if you have a title or a position that grants you power and a certain freedom to act. In this case, you have an even greater responsibility to be a role model for those

> You don't need a title, money or permission to act like a role model for the people around you.

around you. But it is not a necessity. A position as an executive or a business owner only gives you the big privilege to officially apply the philosophy in this book. However, it also works without it.

The End of Excuses

We live in exciting times. Never has it been so easy to be successful. And never has it been so hard to adjust to the increasingly fast change. For this reason, many people prefer to "play it safe". They would rather wait and hide behind rules, hierarchical structures and the most famous expression when it comes to resisting change, "We've never done it this way!" And before you know it, you've got a little bit more comfortable in your comfort zone and keep managing the beloved status quo day after day. But to actively start implementing changes, it is necessary that you get over your own conveniences and start focusing on the huge chances and opportunities lying in every change.

Does this mean you should be fading out all of your problems from now on? No, quite the opposite. You should acquire a taste for a fact pretty quickly. The world is not fair and life is certainly not all guns and roses. There are many obstacles that stand in your way, that challenge you anew every day and put you to the test to see how serious you really are about your goals and dreams. I wish that it was different, but it is what it is. This, too, is one of those facts that we generally cannot change. So let's focus on things that are within our realm of influence instead. And there are a lot of them.

If you have read my previous books, then you will know that I am convinced that life is either black or white. You can either change or stay the way you are. You can decide for or against something. You can take responsibility or become a victim of external circumstances. Believing so little in gray areas is an inevitable side effect of my own personal development process. The more you think and act like a Changemaker the less you will have a desire to deal with the usual back and forth. Instead, you will immediately take a liking to the feeling of satisfaction, which you will inevitably experience the more you commit yourself.

The path that lies before us starts with such a decision. Especially when the external circumstances are hard, the road is rocky and risk is high; you are standing at a fundamental crossroads. Do you flee into passiveness and look for excuses and reasons why you really can't change anything, or do you muster up your courage and become a Changemaker who actively changes himself as well as his surroundings? Who takes responsibility, even when destiny doesn't bode so well at the moment. Who commits to his goals and dreams, even though the road is full of obstacles. Who makes courageous decisions, even though the stakes are high. As I'm writing these lines, I am well aware of how innocent these statements sound when they are written on paper. But don't be deceived, because the practical impact could not be any greater. The decision, whether you are someone who hesitates or someone who commits, will set the course for your future, professionally as well as personally.

The obvious choice is the presumed easier one. You decide to take the path of least resistance, and do what everyone else does. You get way too comfortable in your comfort zone and come to terms with the fact that the circumstances are hard and the future outlook is grim. And just to make sure, you also talk yourself into believing that nothing works anyhow, without a title, money or the permission of others. Then this attitude is dressed up in various excuses, which you use to convince yourself that staying in your comfort zone is the right thing to do.

If you go through life with open eyes, you will soon realize just how colorful the variations of excuses can be. Sometimes they are worded in a very open way, sometimes they are concealed, and, then again, very subtle. And you will observe, again, that people will display a passionate creativity when it comes to finding an excuse to prevent an implementation. A mentor of mine from back when I worked in retail said to me many years ago, "Grzeskowitz, remember one thing, you will be able to apply it your entire life. Those who don't want to do something will look for excuses and reasons why it just won't work. And those who really want something will always find a solution." And right he was. I have the privilege to be working on different changes with people, organizations and companies every day. The topics are very

> Changemakers don't use excuses. They take responsibility for their successes, as well as their failures.

different; but one thing always remains the same: The way of the excuses.

Of course, these people would never admit that they are using excuses to justify their passive life in the comfort zone and to soothe their conscience. Instead, they speak about being realistic, claim that things are just the way they are, or that they just aren't as lucky as other people. But at the end of the day, these verbal smokescreens are nothing more than excuses not to take action and not to make the necessary changes happen. How can I be so sure about this? Why can I assert this so distinctively? Simple. I've used most of these excuses myself. Not only once, but over many, many years. And during my daily work as a speaker, motivational trainer and change managment coach, I keep hearing different variations and many different forms. Even when nothing seems to work anymore, there's always time for a polished excuse in the end.

The big dilemma with this is that most people don't even notice anymore when they are using one of the typical excuses. They've told themselves these things so many times that they start accepting them as a deep and unwavering truth at some point. And it happens so fast. Even I catch myself, at times, wanting to reach for a classic excuse during an idea, an argument or an upcoming change. Thankfully, I also practice the ability of critical thinking, so I usually notice it when it happens. And then I make a conscious choice to take full responsibility.

The key for the transformation of a hesitating attitude into a formative *Think it. Do it. Change it.* mentality is the awareness of the status quo. Only if you know how many times you reach for excuses instead of doing something are you able to change something about it. So at this point, I'd like to invite you to take an honest look into the mirror and check how many times you fall into the mental trap of saying, "We've always done it this way, why should I change anything?" instead of taking responsibility. And believe me, excuses are lurking everywhere. Most of the time they sound so harmless and familiar that we don't even notice them anymore.

But they are present. Every single day. In almost every situation in life. Last year, I asked the readers of my blog to help me start the biggest collection of excuses in the world. At this point, the list contains almost 200 excuses, and it would be great if it could grow even more. (I look forward to your top excuses: http://www.grzeskowitz.de/das-ende-der-ausreden-ein-manifest/) Reading the comments of my readers, it became apparent to me how often I encounter a certain type of excuse in my daily life, how much people inhibit themselves with them and sabotage their own success. To give you a little taste of this, I would like to introduce to you my personal top ten of the most common excuses.

The ten most common excuses that you keep encountering in daily life

1. I don't have any money.
2. I'm too young/old/small/big/etc.
3. This is happening way too fast/slow for me.
4. I don't have time.
5. We've never done it this way.
6. I lack the talent.
7. I'm aware of this/I know this/I know how to do this already.
8. Yes, but...
9. It's not that easy.
10. This will never work.

Heard those before? Maybe even used them yourself? No worries, we all use one or the other excuse on a regular basis. It's far more important that you become aware of what kind of an impact they have on you, because the bottom line is excuses are used so that you do not have to take action, make decisions and continue keeping up the status quo. They encourage you to keep waiting for the right moment. That special instance, when everything is just right. But that moment will never come because something is always amiss.

So, before you make an important decision, you need to be absolutely clear about one thing: The perfect moment does not exist. You will always be acting in a state where you aren't perfectly prepared and you lack knowledge, ability or information. And that's the tragic thing about hesitation. We are just waiting for those perfect circumstances that only exist in theory, and that we will never attain anyway. The results: Waiting. Pushing things off. Finding excuses. And the more comfortable you make your own comfort zone, the harder it becomes to get the results you want. And this is tragic. Just as former German president Gustav Heinemann stated over

> The perfect moment does not exist. The *Think it. Do it. Change it.* mentality will help you with tough decisions.

15

seventy years ago, "Those who are not willing to change things will also lose what they tried to keep in the end."

Stop waiting and make the conscious decision to declare an end to all these excuses. With each excuse that you don't apply anymore, you gain back a piece of your personal responsibility and say goodbye to the victim mentality that's so prevalent these days. It might be unfamiliar at first, and sometimes even hard, because the more independence you gain from your external circumstances the more you are going to reach your personal limits. This is a good thing, because you can only grow and improve on this fine line between success and failure. And nobody is asking you to behave like a robot and cut out all your emotions.

Whenever you're in a situation where everything seems to go against you, it is totally human to be sad, mad or frustrated. You should allow these feelings and appreciate them. But the important thing is not to get caught up in a whirlwind of negativity, but instead start looking ahead again and ask yourself what lesson life wants you to learn at that moment. True to the motto, "Fall down, get back up, fix your crown and move on." Are you ready for the end of excuses? Awesome, but be aware that you have just opened Pandora's box. Once you have tried the precious nectar of personal responsibility, you won't ever want to try anything else.

The *Think it. Do it. Change it.* mentality

There once was a forty-year-old bachelor who still lived at home with his father. One evening, at dinner, his dad made an announcement. He said, "Listen, son, I'm sick. I don't feel well and my time is running out. Maybe I've got another three or four years left. You are the only person I have. When I'm gone, you will inherit my company as well as assets to the amount of a hundred million dollars."

So the son decided to find himself a wife who he could share his future wealth with. And one day, at the airport during a business trip, he met the most beautiful woman he had ever seen. She was so amazing that she nearly took his breath away. But he approached her anyway and said, "My lady, I may look like an ordinary man, but my father will die in three or four years, and then I will inherit his company and also his assets to the amount of a hundred million dollars. Here is my business card."

With a mysterious smile, the woman took the card and left. But before she reached the door, she turned around and said just one sentence. "We will see each other again." And she kept her word. The very next day she became his stepmother.

I don't know about you, but I always have to smile about this little anecdote. Still, there's a very serious point to this story. The message is clear. Don't wait until it's too late, but jump at opportunities when they present themselves. Sadly, this intention is often torpedoed by the rapidly spreading disease number one. What do I mean by that? I'm talking about the famous procrastination. The symptoms are always the same. Instead of initiating change, you'd rather wait and justify this with various excuses. And then you wait. And wait even more. Until the cows come home and someone else took the chance and seized the opportunity.

Saying goodbye to this hesitating wait-and-see attitude and ringing in the end of excuses is therefore a very important step. But it's far from enough. You need an alternative to your former behavior patterns, A *Think it. Do it. Change it.* mentality that focuses on recognizing chances, seizing opportunities and implementing changes. It might take a little bit of time until you can free yourself from the old patterns and conditioning, but it is worth it. And the training is pretty simple. Replace the old reflex with a new one. Where you used to hesitate, doubt and reach for a good old excuse, stop for a moment and think or say very consciously: "Just do it!" Need a few suggestions?

Don't wait, just do it!

- Don't wait until your boss is asking you to, but go the extra mile for your customer now: "Just do it!"
- Don't wait for a co-worker to take care of something, but take on the task yourself: "Just do it!"
- Don't wait for your customers to find you, but pick up the phone: "Just do it!"
- Don't wait until New Years to change your habits, but start today: "Just do it!"
- Don't wait until other people approach you in situations of conflict. Take the initiative yourself: "Just do it!"

- Don't wait for the perfect moment, but take action now: "Just do it!"
- Don't wait until you have a title, enough money or the permission of others. Start changing your life today: "Just do it!"
- Don't wait until the cows come home, but say it loud and clear: "I'm just going to do it!"

This is the *Think it. Do it. Change it.* mentality that will transform you from a world champion of excuses into the world champion of taking action. This is the can-do attitude that will replace hesitation with action. This is the mindset that will keep you at the wheel of the business and make it possible to create your career, your relationships and your life according to your own visions. In the following chapters we will look at the most important ingredients that you will need to integrate this *Think it. Do it. Change it.* mentality into your everyday life.

First, the right motivation helps you to not constantly have to think about your drive, but to concentrate on using upcoming changes to grow and improve as a person. Following this, we will walk along the path of the

> A can-do attitude helps you to design your future according to your own values and principles.

Changemaker and develop strategies that will make you overcome doubt, insecurity and fear of change and make courageous decisions instead. You will learn why the renaissance of values will ensure that you will always have a powerful navigation system for your life at your disposal, which, together with the right intentions, turns you into the best version of yourself. Based on these principles, we will look at two words that have the potential to change your life and why New York is sometimes right around the corner.

Each building block of the *Think it. Do it. Change it.* mentality will be connected by a common theme: The irrefutable decision to take full responsibility for your career, your satisfaction and your quality of life. To no longer rely on other people to tell you what you should think, do or change, but to take action yourself. To no longer wait for the perfect moment, but make the title of this book your daily mantra: *Think it.Do it.Change it.*

Does this sound interesting? You don't need any unique talents, special knowledge or extraordinary abilities to implement all this. Much more important is a high operational readiness and the constant willingness to give just a little bit more than is absolutely necessary. But please allow me a short, but very important remark. Just by reading this, you won't go from hesitating to doing it. It is a rocky road that requires hard work from you, as well as courage and commitment. But every single step is worth these efforts. Is it going to work in any case? I can't say it quite as well as Clint Eastwood, who once stated, "If you want a guarantee, buy a toaster."

Are you ready despite it all? Wonderful, because, as soon as you stop waiting, you will positively influence not only your own life, but also your company, your family and your environment with your personality. And you can start this immediately. Most likely, you've read a book or two of this kind before and you are used to many exercises, tasks and questionnaires waiting for you, the reader, as you go along. I purposely left these things out. For one, I know that almost nobody really completes these tasks (am I right?), and on the other hand, you can start your first step toward personal responsibility immediately.

I really recommend making this book into a personal workbook for yourself. Take notes, dog-ear some pages, highlight areas that are especially inspirational to you and write down your thoughts as often as possible. Written words not only possess an enormous power, but also ensure necessary clarity and get your creative juices flowing. Reading lets you understand, but only writing highly strengthens the effect on your personal development. But think about it; these suggestions, like any other idea in this book, are just an offer. Nobody will force you to do this, and nobody checks up on you. If you don't do it out of your own free will, nothing is going to happen. And this applies as well here: If you don't get it done, nobody will do it for you. So keep thinking about your mantra while reading *Think it.Do it.Change it.*

In exchange for your commitment, I am going to do everything in my power to ensure you take away as much as possible from this reading, for your career, your business and your relationships with other

> Say, "I'm just going to do it!" and start your own change journal.

people. To do this, I am going to shake up the border of your comfort zone as many times as I can. I am going to challenge you with big ideas, which will make you experience insecurity, doubt and fear. Every time you feel these emotions, this is a good sign, because it doesn't mean anything other than you are making progress and are on your way to growing as a person. Therefore, I want to end this chapter with a quote by Ayn Rand, who I admire a great deal. She said, "The question isn't who is going to let me; it's who is going to stop me." And this is one of those thoughts that are worth thinking about a little more intensively.

Chapter Summary

Think it. Do it. Change it. The big ideas of this chapter

- ✓ Actively create change, instead of passively waiting
- ✓ Successful change is not subject to a title, money or the permission of others
- ✓ Don't wait for the perfect moment, just get started
- ✓ Focus exclusively on the things you can control
- ✓ Change, before you get changed
- ✓ Set the pin number for your own life
- ✓ Always be prepared and focus on chances and possibilities
- ✓ Take on full responsibility for your life
- ✓ Announce the end of excuses
- ✓ Let the *Think it. Do it. Change it.* mentality be the guide to your life
- ✓ Say, "I'm just going to do it!" as often as you can

Unleash your Inner Motivation to Change - Why Tschakka Tschakka Is a Thing of the Past

"They were hiding behind hay bales. They were planting in the full moon. They had given all they had for something new. But the light of day was on them. They could see the thrashers coming. And the water shone like diamonds in the dew."

- Neil Young, Thrasher

A few years ago, I was booked for a change consulting in a medium sized company. Right from the beginning, I noticed that the executives of this company had subscribed to the old and famous *wait-and-see-method*. For years, they had been waiting for the right moment to arrive, to begin with the necessary restructuring of the company and to establish a culture in which change isn't viewed as a threat but as the fastest possible way to adjust to the increasing complexity around us. Because of that behavior, we quickly ended up talking about their motivation. And a single sentence fascinated me so much that I have not forgotten it to this day. One of the department managers that were present made the following statement: "You know, Mr. Grzeskowitz, we've already tried that motivation thing here. It didn't work out."

I thought long and hard about this sentence, because without lasting motivation every change is inevitably destined for failure. And here is the curious thing. Most people know this. But when it comes to dealing with their own drive, they start blocking, look for excuses or openly react with resistance. Why is that? The answer lies in a classic dilemma, because you can compare the right motivation for change with intelligence. Everyone is certain that they have enough of it, but everyone else has a substantial backlog. Science calls this phenomenon the *Above Average Effect*. There are studies that show that over ninety percent of those polled allege that their intelligence is above average. But common sense tells us that this equation can't be accurate, right? Relating to our subject, this leads to the following dilemma. Everyone wants change, but nobody wants *to* change. Everyone is convinced that they are highly motivated, but the people around them definitely have to work on it.

But if we regularly pass off responsibility to others, nothing will ever happen. And it's important that we critically question our own attitude as well. I don't know about you, but sometimes I have trouble motivating myself. There are days when I really don't want to do any accounting, can't really get going working on my books, and would rather order a pizza than cook something healthy. And if I look at my daily work with companies, executives and managers, by no means does it seem like I'm the only one. No other topic has had as much time, energy and money invested into it over the years as employee motivation has. It's not surprising, because most companies have already realized that being able to manage change in times of constant shifts has become the number one competitive advantage of the future. And without the right motivation, it will be impossible to constantly adjust to the changing circumstances and to reinvent yourself on a regular basis.

> Everybody wants change. But nobody wants to change. Does this apply to you as well?

Let's take a closer look. What's behind this concept that plays such a central role in literature, the economy and now even sports? Wikipedia defines motivation as, "The set of motives that lead to a state of readiness." Or, expressed in my simpler words, "Motivation is the drive that mentally and physically gets you from point A to point B."

Both sentences make it clear; motivation always comes into play when we want to, or are forced to, change. Nothing happens on its own. You need some sort of drive to change your way of thinking, make different decisions and act in a different way. You need the right dose of motivation to do the following things:

- Have a career
- Get rich
- Stay healthy
- Lose weight
- Lead an independent life
- Fall in love
- Talk to your dream partner
- Be successful
- Acquire new and keep existing customers
- Work out on a regular basis
- Start your own business

But people struggle with nothing more than they do with lasting and long-term changes. If you think about your own experiences from the past few years, you will realize that the problem is not that the motivation doesn't exist at all. Quite the contrary. We often start with a strong inner drive, but, in the end, we end up quitting at some point or we lower our expectations because the initial fire extinguishes pretty fast and gets taken down by routine tasks, the hustle and bustle or the temptations of daily life. The latest diet, the signing up at the gym or the New Year's resolutions send their love.

Science confirms this personal assessment. In 1995, Professor John P. Kotter conducted a huge study of hundreds of companies of various sizes that were actively conducting change management. He came to the following conclusion: seventy percent of all change projects failed and didn't yield the desired results—or, fatalistically worded, "Two out of three change programs fail." Since then almost twenty years have passed; change has increased massively and become a daily companion. So you would think that our willingness to accept change has increased, right? But even today, studies show that seventy percent of all change projects still fail. Some even estimate numbers higher than this.

It's due to the fact that the old rules have long ceased to apply. The timing of changes doesn't rise in a straight line, but exponentially. Eric Schmidt, the former CEO of Google, made a very impressive statement in 2011. He said, "Today, mankind produces as many ideas, information and data within forty-eight hours, as they did all together from the Stone Age until 2003."

Please let this sentence sink in for a minute. What does this mean for your day-to-day life? The risks increase, but so do the opportunities. Most likely, two young students are sitting in their dorm at this very moment, between a tower of pizza boxes, coming up with the idea for the next Apple, Uber or Airbnb. Never in the past has it been so easy to be successful. And never has it been harder to adjust to the increasingly fast changes. This development, of course, isn't without consequences. Many people simply don't know how they should react to this new complexity. And then they do what they have always done, they fall back on methods, techniques and motivating slogans that are outdated and don't do the modern development any justice. That's too abstract for you? Imagine the following situation: You show up at a Formula One circuit in an old 1982 Ford Taurus to compete in a race with Lewis Hamilton, who's sitting next to you in his high-tech Mercedes racing machine and lets his V8 turbo roar with the merest push on the gas pedal. No matter how much you try, you won't have the slightest chance.

Because the world has changed so drastically in the past few years, it is extremely necessary to adapt your ideas, tools and philosophies to this development. Daniel Pink compares the evolution of motivation with regular software updates on the Apple iPhone in his book *Drive – The Surprising Truth That Motivates Us*. I love this metaphor, because the technology giant from Cupertino is a true master in adapting the inner workings of the most successful smartphone of all time to external opportunities, developments and innovations. As soon as there's a technical innovation, Apple reacts and comes out with an upgrade for their operating system. What works well is maintained and complemented with the new requirements. This way, they have been up to date and the famous step ahead of the competition since 2007.

> Take care of your own change projects by taking care of your inner drive.

But while the operating system of the iPhone has developed further through various upgrades from 2007 (iOS 1.0) until today (as I write this chapter, we have reached iOS 9.0.), as far as motivation goes, we came to a standstill somewhere between version 1.0 and 3.0. Many people still use fear and pressure as the alleged motivator number one. Others still swear by a mixture of carrot and stick in the year 2016, while progressive entrepreneurs let their teams walk through fire and chant *Tschakka Tschakka* together. All these methods might even have a short-term effect, but they fall flat in the long term. Additionally, they don't amplify the new complexity, or the modern values of the present day. Therefore, it is about time for a motivation 4.0 upgrade. It is time for a strong inner drive that makes it possible for us to implement changes regardless of titles, money or the permission of others, but with a lot of fun and satisfaction instead. My big goal with this book is for you to unleash inner motivation for change 4.0 and expand it in a way that renders you free from external influences.

Because I've talked about employee motivation so much now, I'd like to make a short statement at this point. I am often asked, "Ilja, are your books geared toward business or more for personal development?" But can you really separate the two areas? Isn't personal development an absolute requirement if we want to have business success? Don't we have to grow our personality first, before we can be a better boss, salesman or business owner? It is one of my deepest beliefs that personal growth and success in your business are inextricably linked to each other.

Because of that, I don't want to have a label put on me. My books are neither B2B (Business to Business), nor B2C (Business to Consumer). They are simply H2H (Human to Human). I write to you as a human, as a fellow human being with all facets, strengths and weaknesses. And one thing I know for sure; the idea of motivation 4.0 will be a good companion for you in all spheres of life. If you are able to give the large and small tasks of everyday life a motivational meaning then you will inevitably feel a growth in success, satisfaction and long-term results. But before we begin to look at each building block a little closer, it is necessary to cut off a few old habits, and say goodbye to a few beloved, but still outdated motivation myths. Would you like to get started?

Motivation 1.0: The Escape from the Sabre-Toothed Tiger

To take a look at the first step in motivational evolution, I would like you to join me in a little thought experiment. Please imagine that we are travelling about 15,000 years back in time. People are living in tribes and have just passed the Neanderthal way of life. While the women are tending to their humble abodes and take care of the children, the men only have one single task: Find food. To do this, they set out, collect berries, hunt mammoths, and often don't return for a few days. What sounds rather romantic to our modern ears was, in reality, a daily struggle of survival. Of course, it also had its good sides. Because if the intensity with which you go about your daily tasks determines if you are alive or dead at the end of the night then you really don't have to worry much about your motivation.

Below the line, our ancestors were primarily led by their instincts. On this intuitive level, they were driven by two basic needs that are still valid today.

1. Reward through the feeling of happiness
2. Avoidance of pain

This is motivation 1.0 in its purest form. But back to our little thought experiment. Feeling happiness back then was almost exclusively equated to interpersonal relationships and a full pot. So the men set out every day to provide their family with enough to eat, regardless of bad weather, illness, or—the then unknown—procrastination that could keep them from this task. If they didn't follow through, the alternative would have been certain death. And that really lurked everywhere back then. Sometimes the hunters and gatherers were so focused on the tasty mammoth during their outings that they didn't notice the sabre-toothed tiger sneaking up behind them. Looking the enemy in the eye, our brave ancestors realized quickly that they'd just found themselves in a fight for their lives. The result was an intensive motivation boost in the form of adrenaline, which made it possible for them to outgrow themselves for a short period of time and escape the sabre-toothed tiger. And that is the second instinctive motivational factor— the avoidance of pain, ensuring your own survival. The people back then did not need more than that.

Surprisingly, the motivational pattern 1.0 has not changed to this day, because it is deeply rooted in our instincts. In modern times, our main motivations certainly are not about life or death anymore, but rather about avoiding pain and seeking happiness. Every individual generally tries to satisfy these two needs. We want to get

> Look out for what makes you happy and what pain you want to avoid.

away from our problems and reach our goal. And let's not fool ourselves, for centuries it was absolutely enough to rely on these two motivational poles and the industrial society was virtually predestined for it. It was not that long ago when executives in a business were exclusively patriarchic and shaped by the "Order de Mufti". Maybe you still remember it as well; the boss gave an order and this order was to be performed. If you didn't do so, or made a mistake, then you had earned yourself some trouble. As far as positive incentives went, one was usually limited to the old German wisdom: "Not complained is praised enough." (And, no, we are not all like that.)

If you object and say that these times are thankfully over, I am going to have to disappoint you. Even today, leadership very often operates with pressure, hierarchical orders and even with fear. The results of this motivational strategy can be observed in the corresponding companies on a daily basis. If an employee is scared of sanctions, the primary instinct that's trying to protect us from pain kicks in. Because of this, he works with the parking brake in place or even does nothing at all to avoid making mistakes. And right away, a virtually unstoppable spiral of standstill, insecurity and resistance sets in that usually influences the climate and the culture of the entire company.

Motivation 2.0: The Carrot and the Stick

The next developmental level of motivational evolution uses the positive sides of the instinctive *Away from the Pain* and *Toward Happiness* and combines them with cognitive elements, such as the reward of desirable and the punishment of undesirable behavior. To stay with the world of metaphors, they entice you with the tasty carrot and threaten with the painful stick. Hang out at a playground on any given afternoon and you can experience this form of motivation in its purest form, "Kevin-Tyron-Jason, if you don't get off the jungle gym immediately, you aren't going to be allowed to watch Sesame Street tonight." Or the goal oriented variation, "Bridget, if you play with Jacqueline for another half hour, Daddy will buy you some yummy ice cream."

Not only for children, but also for us adults, the carrot and stick still work wonders during certain activities. When we reach a desired goal, we reward ourselves with a new pair of shoes, a spa weekend in London or the newest iPhone. And the fear of the stick ensures that we always stay on the ball. We work overtime to be able to afford the next vacation in Florida, so we don't have to endure the disdaining looks of the neighbors, who've owned a villa in Cape Coral for years. We diet to the point of eating disorders because we fear being ridiculed for our gut during our next beach vacation. And if the natural form of the stick is not enough anymore, there are technical gadgets that are supposed to help us reach our goals. This is why the inventor Maneesh Sethi recently introduced his fitness bracelet called *Pavlok*, which gives its users an electric shock if they do not implement his training program rigorously enough. I'm not kidding.

Motivation 2.0 is determined by a classic "If ... Then rule". If we do X then we get a certain reward. If we do not do Y, we are punished by negative sanctions. A good metaphor for that is the donkey who has a tasty, but unattainable carrot held in front of his face while, simultaneously, the painful stick is used to spank his behind in order to get him to run. You probably know this version of motivation 2.0 best from your day-to-day practice at work. Every prospective executive learns at the beginning of their career that a balanced application of carrot and stick is needed for good leadership. An appropriate amount of praise should always stand opposite of the corresponding critique. So, for many years, material and immaterial incentives have been used to entice while threatening with reprimands, relocation or termination at the same time.

The logic behind this is simple. Based on a certain assessment (usually revenue or profit), incentives in the form of bonuses, material assets or privileges are set, which you can add to your base salary depending on the appropriate result. Of course, one would expect a higher motivation with this type of compensation, which results in an equally high commitment and the corresponding efforts. Even in high-performance sports, this kind of drive is the order of the day. Players, team managers and especially the ever-increasing number of agents earn a lot of money, because the club owners have succumbed to the call of the carrot. Take a look at the sports section in the newspaper, and you will see a true plethora of reports about bonus payments. There is prize money, goal bonuses, crown premiums, champion money, non-relegation premiums and, of course, the publicly controversially debated switching bonuses.

Do these incentives have a controlling function? You bet. However, motivation 2.0 by carrot and stick has two fundamental drawbacks. For one, people quickly get used to a certain reward level and want more at some point. They get addicted to rewards and, sooner or later, they don't do anything without one. What was enough last year isn't nearly adequate today. There is a reason why we live in a time of permanent "faster – harder – stronger". And even the best threat wears out if it isn't implemented consistently (and, in practice, this happens almost never).

> Motivation through carrot and stick has its limitations, so use it carefully.

So the first issue with carrot and stick is the threat of attrition and therefore it does not have very strong sustainability. On the other hand, motivation 2.0 is only applicable to behavior patterns that have a concrete and measurable output in dollars, quantities or goals scored per season. But today we are living in times of less and less assembly line work, fewer standardized procedures and one-dimensional job descriptions. Instead, creative and unconventional tasks have increased, which are difficult to measure. Here is a challenge for you. Try to motivate a creative art director, a game designer or an author of change books by providing incentives for his output or threaten him with the stick if he isn't creative enough. If you don't focus on a strong inner drive in these situations, you will soon grit your teeth. And that's where motivation 3.0 comes into play.

Motivation 3.0: Tschakka, you Can Do It!

In the 1990s, the realization prevailed that a motivation that was strictly based on external incentives was not really marked by sustainability. Freethinker and bestselling author Reinhard Sprenger even alleged in his famous book, *The Myth of Motivation*, that all motivational methods practiced in companies are counterproductive. It was the birth of intrinsic motivation, which focused on inner motives to get from point A to point B. At the same time, motivational gurus sprung up like mushrooms, made thousands of people walk over hot coals and set free their inner power in a kind of primal scream therapy. About twenty years have passed since hundreds of thousands of people made a pilgrimage to the motivational temples all over the world to get this special kick for their own career.

In Europe, this time is associated with no other name than the Dutch trainer Emil Ratelband. He gained huge popularity with his slogan *Tschakka, you can do it!* and even spent a few months hosting a show of the same name on German television. Over night, the word *Tschakka* became a kind of battle cry for followers of motivation 3.0 to scream out that you can do anything if you only put your mind to it. And even though it's not his fault, the creator of this made-up word became the symbol for the escalated motivational scene that advertised their ever-growing events with sometimes-questionable methods and gained a pretty dubious reputation. And it gets worse. Upon closer inspection, countless promises by these motivational gurus turned out to be full of one thing: Hot air.

How deeply disillusion stings for some people is something I still notice today when I get booked for motivational keynote speeches by companies or associations. Often I am told during the briefing, "Mr. Grzeskowitz, please don't start with this Tschakka stuff. Our employees react quite allergic to that." It always takes a lot of persuasive power to put my clients at ease and explain that other forms of motivation exist. But even today the sting is deep and the label *motivational speaker* still doesn't carry the best reputation. And this is a shame, because motivation 3.0 in its core contains a bunch of extremely good approaches.

If you have read my previous books then you will know how much I believe in the inner potential of each person and how much I enjoy helping them develop it. But unfortunately, below the line, the statements of many motivational gurus are limited to trivial truisms that are neither true nor work. And there really is a whole cornucopia of them. To verify this statement practically during the research phase for this book, I spontaneously started a request on my Facebook page asking my contacts to tell me the most boring motivational slogan they knew. The result was overwhelming. Within two hours, I got over a hundred comments, with some of the classics you will now get to read. At this point, I would like to critically examine the seven biggest motivational lies of the modern day Tschakka (and esoteric) gurus. Here we go.

Motivational lie #1: You can achieve anything

This famous motivational message managed to dissolve thousands of pipe dreams into thin air. To be honest, it does sound enticing: "It doesn't matter what you do, who you are or what you want to have. If you can dream it, you can do it. You just have to beat on your chest, fervently shout Tschakka, and, like magic, you now can achieve anything." In order to substantiate these empty promises, fluffy, but unfortunately false analogies are being quoted, like the story of the bumblebee who really can't fly but doesn't know this and flies anyway (ever heard that one?). And if you hear these types of statements often enough, you eventually start believing them.

Where these empty promises lead can be observed every Saturday night on TV while watching *American Idol*, where teenagers with a complete lack of talent throw every well-meaning piece of advice from the jury to the wind, and follow their dream of a singing career with a croaky voice. The argument is always the same, "I can't sing, nor am I musical, but every day I imagine myself busting the charts as the new pop sensation. And I can achieve anything I put my mind to."

> You have to accept that everyone has limitations and you can't achieve everything.

You know similar examples, am I right? This makes it very obvious that motivation 3.0 can do more harm than good, if it is misunderstood. And just to make it clear once more, of course every person has much more inside of them than most people can imagine. But that everyone can achieve anything is simply not true. People have limitations, plain and simple, that make some goals unrealistic, per se. I, for example, will never in my life become a gymnast, math professor or concert pianist. Even though I have a positive attitude, strongly believe in myself and am willing to practice a lot, I still will not make it. And that's really not a big deal because I am focused on my individual talents, my strengths and on those areas in my life in which I haven't reached my full potential yet. And you should do the exact same thing. You might not be able to have it all, but you will gain much more than you might imagine today.

Motivational lie #2: The universe will take care of your success

You can't imagine how many people I have had the pleasure to meet who sit on their couch every evening with the book *The Secret* and send one wish after another into the universe. And then they wonder why they still have a job they hate, why their long-term relationship is losing more and more passion and the imagined Porsche in the garage ends up being a rickety Fiat Punto from 1997 upon closer inspection. Even though I believe in the law of attraction, it's time to make one thing clear. No matter what you plan to do, if you aren't willing to take the necessary action, you won't reach your goals. Was this too direct? Maybe, but being successful always means having to work hard for it. To rely on wishing upon the universe, unfortunately, is not enough. And if anyone is telling you anything different, they are plainly and simply lying to you.

Motivational lie #3: Everything is okay just the way it is

Another cheesy line that unfortunately falls on fertile ground too often. It is the best excuse that I know for not trying to change anything. After all, everything is okay just the way it is. And even if you are completely dissatisfied with yourself and the world around you then it just wasn't meant to be. Time for a straight talk. If you are one of those people who have been led to believe this delusion, I have an important message for you. There are times in life when everything is not okay the way it is. If you don't happen to live inside a Rosamunde Pilcher movie, there are periods when you fight with problems, are in trouble or don't know how to deal with all the crap happening to you. By the way, this is called life. And there is only one person who can change these things. That person is looking at you in the mirror every single morning. There is no use at all sticking your head in the sand and saying mean things in beautiful words. Quite the opposite, the beauty in life is the constant up and down; the change from highs to lows. And the sooner you accept this fact the better. More so, be happy about these supposed hard moments, because every problem is a starting point to making a change. The only thing you should never forget is to shift your focus on to possible solutions right away.

Motivational lie #4: You just have to want it, everything else will happen on its own

If a motivational guru wants to make this misbelief tempting to you then he is lying to you. Nothing, absolutely nothing happens on its own. Of course, it is important that you to want to change and take on your project highly motivated. But the desire for it, unfortunately, is only one prerequisite, the necessary precursor for the all-deciding factor—being able to do it. You need knowledge, skills and experience. Not only once, but all the time. You have to read a lot, practice a lot and try a lot, because if you are not a master of your craft, it is impossible to reach respectable results, much less be any good at it.

Motivational lie #5: You have to be authentic

I don't believe in anything as much as I believe in the uniqueness of every single person. Every one of us is very special with individual strengths and weaknesses. But when a guru announces the message that you only have to be authentic on the big motivational stage, this means only one thing for the majority of the listening audience. A cheap excuse, not having to improve or grow as a person. Let's not fool ourselves, we all have a ton of weaknesses and inner conflicts. We all fight our demons. You do, just as well as I do. You have to work on them, and eventually turn them into strengths. The motivational mantra, "I'm just authentic," is a kind of general absolution to stay exactly the way you are. And best-case scenario, this means standstill, but most of the time it even means taking a step back.

> Have you ever bought into a motivational lie?

Motivational lie #6: Do it with passion or do not do it at all

The distinct obsession with passion has many times led to people quitting their jobs, giving up halfway through, or not starting at all. This is usually only justified with the explanation that the inner passion for something just isn't there (anymore). And let me be absolutely clear about this. I think it is wonderful to be dying for something and I am also a huge fan of passionate actions. This way, power, energy and endurance is set free. But there are also large amounts of tasks in life that just have to get done.

Believe me; when I do my accounting, my passion level is down to exactly zero. But I still get it done because it is necessary. If my dentist performs a root canal, I really don't care about his passion. It is much more important to me that he is concentrating and working diligently. And when

I'm flying from Berlin to New York City, I really don't care if the pilot in the cockpit is living his dream. All that matters is that he flies me and the other passengers to our destination safely. Most jobs and occupations simply aren't very sexy or exotic, but based on routines, diligence and reliability. Only when we manage to make these characteristics the basis of our daily lives are we able to use the power of our passion for the bigger responsibilities.

Motivational lie #7: You just have to see things positively

Do you know people who constantly walk through life with rose-colored glasses? They never have any problems and see great possibility everywhere. They laugh about every difficulty and have subscribed to the dogma of positive thinking? I meet a lot of these contemporaries daily. Usually, they're marginally successful and rarely truly satisfied. Of course, I am recommending a positive basic attitude to you, because it makes the crucial difference in where your focus is aimed; but there are times when you have to solve problems, fight challenges that let you grow or make wrong decisions, which you have to learn from. To ignore or deny this is not only counter-productive, but leads to dissatisfaction in the long term. Please realize this one thing; it is perfectly okay to be in a bad mood sometimes and go through hard times. The only important thing is what you do with this situation and how fast you manage to make a solution-oriented decision. If you integrate this mentality into your daily life, you can confidently pack the forced positive thinking into a drawer.

> If your intention is strong, you don't need the motivational Tschakka Tschakka stuff.

Have I disillusioned you a bit with the seven biggest motivational lies, or have you always had the feeling that there was something wrong with most of these modern slogans? Even though there is quite a bit of truth to these statements, most people have a pretty decent feeling for someone trying to pull the wool over their eyes. It's a shame, because nothing is quite as strong as distinctly intrinsic motivation. In the end, it all comes down to the intention with which the core messages of motivation 3.0 are conveyed. When I look around, I notice that more and more people have understood exactly that. They want to use the positive elements of intrinsic motivation for themselves and their lives, but can forgo the empty phrases and Tschakka Tschakka ado. It's time for a paradigm shift. It's time for an upgrade.

Motivation 4.0: Meaningful Change Instead of Empty Phrases

The newest upgrade to motivation 4.0, how I define it in this book, combines the properly working elements of the first three developmental stages and complements them with the requirements that have become necessary in our complex world of increasingly faster changes. The demographic development, the globalization and the transformation to a digital service society have led to a radical change in values that has just started to show its changed implications. Here are a few examples of many. We are changing from a premise-based industrial to a globally networked service society. The classic "nine to five" jobs are losing more and more importance, while creative and individual occupations are increasing. And the classic family divisions where the man earns the money and the woman takes care of the house and the children have also long become obsolete. Job sharing, part-time work and combination of job and family have become more important for the majority of people than ample bonuses, provisions and Christmas checks.

Of course, money is still a very important motivational factor and I enjoy earning a lot of money. But it is not everything. Below the bottom line, completely different values are important today; having the freedom to implement your own personality into your work, the ability to flexibly manage your time or experience a better quality of life overall. The most important currency of modern people in the twenty-first century is not the dollar or the euro anymore, but, plain and simple, time. Not for nothing, the amount of sabbaticals has dramatically increased in the past few years. Nowadays, a professional career and the development of your own individuality simply have to reconcile. For quite a while now, people haven't wanted to sit in an office like worker bees from morning until evening, stand at an assembly line or work in a production hall. Instead, they want to live out their creativity, have a meaningful occupation and substantiate their talents.

Nobody wants to have the feeling of having wasted their own potential at the end of their life. And because that's how it is, nobody wants to state on their deathbed, "I regret not having spent more time at the office." In the year 2016 it just has to be possible to live your dreams and express your own personality through your job. Motivation 4.0 captures exactly this trend. It focuses on the highest drive that you could possibly have: When what you do or are has a purpose. When you feel a strong sense of satisfaction when you come home at night. When you follow your own vision and are part of a mission that is bigger than you. When you feel a profound motivation, for which you don't need a title, money or permission from other people.

The moment that was supposed to decisively change my own life occurred on the day my oldest daughter, Emma, was born. I will never forget the emotional wave that overcame me when I was the first person in the delivery room to hold this beautiful baby after a long and strenuous birth. Feeling the strains, she was resting on my chest, wrapped in a cozy towel, and was looking at me with bright eyes. And in that moment I had a feeling like I had been hit with full force by a baseball bat that was made exclusively out of love. With shaking knees and misty eyes, I felt the unconditional affection that you can probably only comprehend if you have children yourself.

From one moment to the next, my entire worldview had been turned upside down and this changed everything. It seemed to me as though everything around me was moving in slow motion; while a deep realization came over me at the same time about what is really important in life. I felt an unprecedented responsibility towards this little girl; rose to the challenge and solemnly promised her I would do anything in my power to give her the best life possible.

However, to put this promise into action I had to first free myself from the visible and invisible chains of my own life; move away from the heteronomy and into taking a hundred percent responsibility for my career, my decisions and my actions. If I wanted to be there for my daughter, I myself would have to decide what the future was going to look like. Nobody else. And so I decided, in this moment in the delivery room, to release the parking brake and finally, completely unleash my own potential. To not only understand this *Think it. Do it. Change it.* mentality intellectually, but to live it every single day. To start on the path to my own greatness. This was necessary, because I didn't

> Choose a job that lets you express your personality and use your talents.

want a mediocre life for Emma, but an extraordinary life, at every level. And I threw myself at this task like I had never thrown myself at any task before.

And another thing became very clear to me. I had to turn thirty years old to completely understand how much your own motivation starts to grow once you start acting. And even though I did not know back then how my future path was going to look, I just got started. The basic direction was clear to me and I had faith that the details would work themselves out on the way. When the *why* is strong enough, the how and the *what* just follow automatically. And whenever I started feeling doubt, if I had to move a huge rock out of the way, or overcome an obstacle, one look at my little girl's picture was enough to give me the motivation to continue.

Today, ten years later, I know that a strong drive is the most important prerequisite to replace a passive wait-and-see attitude with determined actions and live changes with heart and soul. I also know that many people are desperately searching for this strong *why*, and simply have no idea what they should be waking up for every morning. I receive requests from people on a regular basis, asking me to support them in finding their strong drive through coaching. This, however, is a big challenge, because a strong *why* never comes from the outside. You can't make it, you can't force it and you can't buy it either. Instead, you are just going to feel it when there is something in your life that makes your eyes light up and your heart beat faster.

For me, that something was the birth of my first child. For others it's a step up the corporate ladder, the acknowledgement of an honorary position, the relationship to a special person or the founding of their own business. It could be something else entirely. And rarely does it stay with this one strong why. I've been lucky to have encountered so many intense experiences on my path that I have multiple strong drives today. My productive work as an independent entrepreneur, the change in my audience after a speech or the feedback from the readers of my books makes me wake up thankful every single morning and helps me to go about my alleged routine chores highly motivated.

But as much as I enjoy being able to travel around the world, speak in exciting companies and work with outstanding personalities, nothing compares to the status my two children have in my life. Nothing fulfills me more than being able to spend an afternoon with Emma and Elisabeth, to laugh and goof off with them, and just watch them enjoy their lives. Since I've gotten to know this feeling, I have never, ever had to waste a single thought on my why or my motivation.

This brings me to the deciding question. What does your strong *why* look like? What makes you jump out of bed full of joy in the morning? What is your drive that lets you get back up after you fall, and gets you closer to your goal, step by step? If you don't have an answer right away, it's's not a big deal at all. It might just be the fact that, over the years, you've learned to focus on the things that you think you're lacking. Exciting things start to happen as soon as you start sharpening your view on the things you already have. And those are more than you might think.

> What fills your heart with joy? When your why is strong enough, the how and what will follow automatically.

Deeply listen to your inner voice. Sooner or later, you will understand, feel and especially know what the strong *why* is in your life. And then it's really happening. Of course, such an inner drive doesn't just appear from one day to the next. It requires a lot of self-reflection, a ton of hard work and, of course, endurance. But it is worth it, because once you start to feel a motivation that is mostly independent from external factors, you will feel a deep fulfillment. And there is more, because you won't want to wait to start making the changes in your life that you have dreamt about for so long. I could never say it as well as the Dalai Lama, who once said, "If our motivation is strong and healing, we can do anything." With this in mind, let us take the next step.

Chapter Summary

Think it. Do it. Change it. The big ideas of this chapter

- ✓ Motivation is the drive that gets you from point A to point B physically and mentally
- ✓ Motivation 1.0 has two forms of drive: Reward through the experience of happiness and the avoidance of pain
- ✓ Motivation 2.0 is backed my the tasty carrot and the painful stick

---

- ✓ Don't be fooled by the motivational lies of motivation 3.0 and develop your own strong, intrinsic motivation
- ✓ Motivation 4.0 combines the efficient elements of the first three developmental stages, and complements them with the necessary requirements in times of change
- ✓ The biggest motivation develops when you spring into action and lead a meaningful life

---

The Path of the Changemaker –
Why You Should Start Doing It

"Never win and never lose. There's nothing much to choose. Between the right and wrong. Nothing lost and nothing gained. Still things aren't quite the same. Between you and me. I keep a close watch on this heart of mine."

- John Cale, I Keep a Close Watch

Can I make a confession? I love reading newspapers like *USA Today*, *The Sun* or Germany's *Bild*. Every time I enter an airport lounge, I reach straight for one of these influential tabloids. This has two reasons. For one, all three of them have the best sports sections of all newspapers by far. But especially fascinating to me are the headlines that literally draw the reader into the paper. Nobody else quite manages to summarize the feeling of an entire nation in a few simple words. And, to be honest, when *Bild* published the headline "We are the pope!" (after the election of Joseph Aloisius Ratzinger as Pope Benedikt XVI.) in 2005, most Germans felt quite a bit pontifical.

Because of my weakness for the suction effect of languages, I have dealt with the headlines of my books a bit more intensively in the past few years. But when I decided on *Think it. Do it. Change it. How to Dream Big, Act Bold and Get the Results You Want* in this case, I started to have doubts. Of course, these words can hold a distinct power, which will hopefully provide you with courage, is contagious and prompts realization. But at the same time I kept asking myself what else could be added to this sentence. *Think it. Do it. Change it.* says all there is to say, right? Message explained, message understood, message realized. So why write an entire book about it?

The answer lies in a small, but often forgotten, detail when it comes to taking chances and actively creating your own future. Because change is one of those things. Everyone knows that it is necessary, and everyone also knows how it works in theory. But then why do so many change efforts fail? Of course, I could point to one of the many change models, which all more or less say exactly the same thing in a complicated way. But I believe the reason is much simpler that that. Most changes fail because it is human to hold on to old habits; because changes can't be automated, can't be delegated and especially can't be bought. Because change isn't what happens on the outside, but the way you deal it within the six inches between your ears. And with that, I certainly mean your mind, but even more your heart.

Have you ever heard of Clocky? Clocky is an alarm clock on wheels, invented by American student Gauri Nanda at MIT in Cambridge, Massachusetts. And with her invention, she has solved an important motivational problem. Maybe you know what I'm talking about. Before you go to bed, you make a rational decision and set your alarm clock for six am, so that you have enough time for a morning run or for a nice long breakfast. The plan is in place and you are really determined. But then it happens. When the alarm clock rings early in the morning, your emotions take over and suddenly there is nothing more important than staying in your warm and comfy bed for another five minutes. And without even noticing it, you reach out your arm, hit the snooze button and say to yourself, "But tomorrow I will definitely get up early!" Clocky doesn't let you do that. When it rings, Clocky falls from your bedside table, and, with an annoying sound, it moves through your bedroom so that you are forced to run after your alarm clock in your underwear. And just in case you are thinking, *Who on Earth needs such an alarm clock?* in the first two years after its invention, without any marketing at all, 35.000 units of Clocky were sold at a price of fifty dollars. Clocky solves the problem when logic wants one thing but the emotions want something entirely different.

But we desperately need both for successful changes. The most in-depth information, the most detailed data and the most profound analyses won't do a thing for you if you don't have any emotional drive. Logic lets you understand, and emotions let you take action. You can check this very easily. Most people know that they should eat healthier. Most people know that they should exercise more. But exceedingly few change their ways. I, for example, know that it would look absolutely amazing if I walked around with a six pack during my next beach vacation. I know about a plethora of books, have all the necessary information and I know exactly what I would have to do to get one. But I don't have a six pack because my emotional drive isn't strong enough. It is one of those changes where you say, "Would be nice, should be done, I should get on it."

I experience the same dilemma on a regular basis during my work with companies and executives in order to develop their ability to transform their ideas into actions. The necessary steps are so simple that anyone would internalize and understand them rationally in a short period of time. But if this logical understanding isn't backed by emotional components, the announced change is nothing more than lip service. And

> You need a rational and an emotional drive in order to change. Logic lets you think and feelings let you take action.

believe me, in this case I don't only speak as a mentor, but from my own experiences. There was a time in my life when I understood the *Think it. Do it. Change it.* mentality inside and out, but was walking a very thin line emotionally. In the back of my head, I always had the feeling that I needed a title, money or the permission of my superiors.

Only in hindsight did I realize that this exact way of thinking was an easy excuse for me, so I could keep driving on with the parking brake firmly in place. When in doubt, I could hide behind company politics, the decisions of my superiors or the countless regulations of the office bureaucracy. This was not without consequences. Looking from the outside in, I was pretty successful, but inside of me, a familiar feeling started to nag, which got louder and louder every day, telling me that this couldn't be it. I felt more and more that it was due time to release the knot and exploit my own potential. And that's when the moment came, in which my intellectual way of thinking was combined with a never-before-seen wave of emotions, and the realization hit me like a brick that I don't need a title, money or permission to live exactly the life that I've always dreamt about. All of a sudden, I had intense clarity and knew: *It is all up to me. I just have to implement it. I have to walk down the path of the Changemaker.*

Being a Leader Is Not a Title, but an Attitude

So what exactly is a Changemaker? For me, it's those people who combine courageous ideas with clear actions and view the various challenges of everyday life as a beautiful gift of life. Those who focus on the big chances and opportunities and actively mold their future. Those who don't change just for the sake of the changes, but are willing to grow as a person and get better every single day. Those who forgo well-meaning announcements and rather focus on letting actions speak. Those who do well when it comes down to acting like a role model for their colleagues, co-workers, customers, friends and family members. In short: Changemakers are those people who make the decision to put their own personal stamp on life and leave the world just a tiny bit better than they found it.

With this short definition, you can undoubtedly tell that this doesn't pertain to a title or a hierarchical position, but a very special can-do attitude. And because that's the way it is, you can divide the people around you into two categories: The Changemakers and the Status Quo Managers. You can find the prime examples, including mixes between the two, everywhere, in your company, your social circle and in your sports club. Let us take a closer look at the typical characteristics of both lifestyles.

> A Changemaker wants to leave the world a tiny bit better that he found it.

A Status Quo Manager

- Sees changes as a threat
- Fears the unknown
- Thinks he knows and is familiar with everything
- Reacts passively to outside circumstances
- Is looking for excuses and reasons why something just doesn't work
- Is problem oriented
- Would rather sit back and do nothing instead of making a mistake
- Does not like to make decisions
- Hides behind rules
- Changes his opinions and values to appeal to others

- Accepts the status quo as a given and not changeable
- Does not take on responsibility
- Hides behind other people

A Changemaker

- Sees changes as a huge opportunity to grow, to learn and improve
- Follows the concept of lifelong learning
- Actively creates his outside circumstances
- Finds ways and means to put his plans into action
- Is solution oriented
- Is ready to make mistakes to be able to learn from them
- Makes punctual, clear and relatable decisions
- Is willing to break rules and replace them with his own
- Lives according to well established values
- Questions everything, especially his own opinions and judgments
- Takes responsibility for himself and his actions
- Acts with intention
- Leads with personality

Did you recognize yourself or someone in your environment in these statements? I hope this short summary made it clear, once again, that the big difference between a Status Quo Manager and a Changemaker does not lie in his talents, his abilities or external circumstances. It's not a question of hierarchical positions either. I know Changemakers that earn their bacon as clerks, secretaries and bus drivers. And, by the same token, I know politicians (lots of them), executives and CEOs that are prime examples of a Status Quo Manager. No, the deciding difference lies in a very special attitude; to take your fate into your own hands, actively create change, as well as taking responsibility for yourself and for others. Therefore, Changemakers are always leaders that the people around them can orient themselves by. And the clearer their own ideas, values and opinions are, the easier it is for their co-workers, colleagues or customers to simply follow suit. To achieve this, it is necessary to internalize four attributes and make them part of your daily routine. These are—as usual—very easy to understand, but not quite as easy to apply.

Changemaker attribute #1: Take responsibility

I know you are probably sick of this statement already, but it is so essential and important that I don't mind bringing it up yet again. If you want to say goodbye to your passive wait-and-see approach then you cannot avoid this step. The alternative is to let the direction, way and speed of your life be determined by other people. But then you will never feel the deep and intense satisfaction that only appears when you take responsibility for your own decisions, your actions and your results.

And, of course, this is hard sometimes, takes a lot of courage and often you will feel like the loneliest person on the planet. You have to make it clear to yourself that changes always go hand in hand with risks, insecurity and fear of the unknown. But as tough as the external circumstances may seem sometimes, you still have the opportunity to turn them into something positive. When the storm is blowing directly into your face you

> Overcome the passive wait-and-see approach and become a Changemaker.

should recall the most important fact. You cannot change what happens to you. But you always have a choice in how you deal with it.

Changemaker attribute #2: Learn to make decisions

Nothing is more important for the right motivation to change than the ability to be able to make decisions. (How to best go about this is detailed in the chapter entitled "Use your Uniqueness." Why is the world so full of mediocracy, complaining and whining? Because so many people are afraid to make mistakes, and therefore choose not to make any decisions at all. The result? Apathy, standstill and many times even regression. Train yourself as often as you can in making clear and punctual decisions. This way you take a stand, convince with confidence and relay values to your environment so that other people can orient themselves accordingly.

Changemaker attribute #3: Go First!

This is one of the most important of these four attributes. *Always Go First.* The great Mahatma Gandhi once said, "Be the change you want to see in the world." Translated into more modern language, this means: Live the changes and change yourself first and foremost. If you want to improve communications in your team, you have to change your ways of communicating first. If you want your employees and colleagues to be more motivated, you have to motivate yourself first. If you want your environment to change, you have to first change yourself.

Changes follow a simple logic. If we change ourselves, everything around us will change as well. But for this it is necessary that we do not expect anything from someone that we wouldn't be willing to do ourselves. With this, you give your co-workers, colleagues and customers clear direction. You create trust and credibility. The more actively you apply the concept of *Always Go First,* the less you are a puppet of external circumstances. If you hold the key to action in your own hands, you leave nothing up to chance, especially in insecure times, and are always the one crucial step ahead of your fate because you are always prepared, actively take action and initiate change without a title, money or permission.

Changemaker attribute #4: Let your actions speak louder than words

An old Chinese proverb says, "I cannot understand your words. Your actions scream so loudly." I keep meeting people who promise the most beautiful things with empty words in terms of what they plan to do, what goals they are following and what they definitely want to achieve. Most of the time, it doesn't get past these announcements and, instead of consequent implementation, their energy is wasted on looking for excuses to explain why it's just not working out. As a Changemaker you let actions speak instead of words. You forgo big announcements, and just do it. You thrill your co-workers, colleagues and customers with your competence in achieving and prefer to leave the verbal boasting to others.

You like these four attributes? Great! They will build the foundation when you follow the path of the Changemaker. They are a kind of a general guideline, to celebrate long-desired successes and directly achieve feasible results. No matter what challenge awaits you in the future, take on responsibility, learn to make decisions, actively apply the principle of *Always Go First* and enthrall with your high competence to achieve. Stop waiting and change your immediate environment, even without a title, money or permission from others. With consequent application, you will soon notice that you are growing as a person and your general satisfaction is rising. But you will also most likely notice that your own demands are growing as well. What seemed unattainable yesterday could be the new standard tomorrow. The more you reach the borders of your comfort zone, the more these will expand. Thus, don't rest on your own laurels but let the daily work on your own development become a subconscious automatism. For this is it necessary to say goodbye to a few dearly beloved ways of thinking.

> "Be the change you want to see in the world." (Gandhi)

Stop Sabotaging yourself

Maybe you know that feeling. Your job isn't what it once was anymore, the long-term relationship is missing a bit of spark, and your bank account is empty in the middle of the month already. There is only once choice. You have to make a change. But while Changemakers are taking action on their plans, the Status Quo Managers take a wait-and-see approach. And if they happen to spring into action more or less by chance, they usually fall right back into their old behavioral patterns. But what is the reason for this? It's possessing neither the will, nor the necessary skills nor the desire to actually make a change.

No, most people want nothing more than to have a demanding job, a satisfying relationship or happy life. But as soon as they have made the decision to take the first step, they start sabotaging themselves. And the tragic thing is that most of them aren't even aware that they are getting in their own way. Instead they convince themselves that they don't have any luck, never had a fair chance or it's just not the right moment. These are just examples of a very special way of thinking that is responsible for our sabotaging ourselves from implementing a desired change. But it doesn't have to be this way. Quite the contrary. Every single human being can become a Changemaker. And the most important step is to drop the following thinking patterns immediately.

Self-Sabotaging-Pattern #1: Being afraid of change

Whether it is about your business or your family life, every change is neutral in itself. It's always our personal evaluation that makes the corresponding event a positive or a negative one. So, truth be told, how do you react when you have to deal with new ideas, ways of thinking or situations? Do you see change as a threat or as a wonderful opportunity to develop your personality, grow your business and make exciting experiences? No matter what your dreams look like, if you are afraid of the necessary changes, it will be hard to make them come true. Instead, you should consider that the opportunity of going new ways is a huge gift in life and it is perfectly normal to feel a bit insecure and have some doubts. If you don't have these feelings then you can be sure that your endeavor is not big enough. And please, never forget one thing. Being courageous doesn't mean having no fear. Being courageous means starting anyway. And we will look at how exactly this is done in the next chapter, when we deal with the subject of fear more extensively.

Self-Sabotaging-Pattern #2: Focus on problems

Where your focus goes, your time, money and energy will also go. We get more of what we concentrate on. This applies to every single area in life. If you expect problems everywhere then you will pull them into your life. If you shift your focus on to chances and opportunities instead, all of a sudden you will notice them everywhere. According to the motto, "The question is not if life is beautiful, but if you are aware of it." In every situation, you have the choice of what to focus on—whether to be the kind of person who constantly whines, complains, and expects a dark cloud on the most beautiful sunny day, or to focus on possible solutions. The tricky thing with this kind of self-sabotage is that we don't see it that way, because this thinking pattern has long become normal. Let me give you an example.

Recently, I received a call from the regional manager of a pretty big company and he said, in a whiny voice, "Mr. Grzeskowitz, I would love to book you for a keynote speech. Our whole industry is doing badly, a brutal price fight is happening, innovations are just not possible anymore, earnings are dropping, politics aren't helping either, the changes have gotten so massive ... yadi yadi yada." I can't really remember the rest, but he went on like this for at least five minutes. And, finally, he said, and he was completely serious, "And you know what the worst thing is? My whole team is constantly complaining, whining and focusing on negative things."

Well, the question of where they learned that behavior answers itself, don't you think? But I experience this kind of attitude on a regular basis. Instead of rolling up the sleeves, one focuses on external circumstances and just keeps up the status quo, in a best-case scenario. And the reasoning is mostly as follows: "What can I do? People just don't want to deal with changes anymore." But I'm going to claim that this is not true. Generally speaking, people like change. You can easily test this if you have kids (or know couples with kids). Do you remember the sleepless nights, the huge pile of diapers and the lovely sound of a baby crying in the middle of the night? I have two wonderful daughters myself, and I don't think it's an exaggeration when I say that the birth of a child is the probably biggest change we can go through, right? And I'm willing to bet that you did initiate this special change on purpose, and at the same time also would rate it as the most beautiful miracle ever. Am I right?

> Awaken the desire to change—in yourself and the people around you.

It's not the change itself that many people are tired of. We love getting promoted, configuring a new car or planning our next vacation; we just don't want to deal with the changes that go along with insecurity, doubt and the fear of the unknown. But if you have adopted the attitude of a Changemaker, even these tough changes can be mastered successfully. The more you train to shift your focus, the more you will notice the many opportunities that life is offering you. And then you just have to grab and use them.

Self-Sabotaging-Pattern #3: Blaming others

Life isn't always how we want it to be and sometimes things happen that we don't like. And the ones to blame are quickly found. Your boss is an unfair slave driver, your employees are a lazy bunch, your spouse is egoistical, your kids are unappreciative, politicians are self-indulgent and the IRS greedy. And because that's how it is, you always know exactly who and what around you has to change, so that you can stay exactly the way you are. Sound familiar? If you have a tendency to immediately blame others when undesired results occur, I'd like to encourage you to definitely try something different. Anyway, it's impossible to change other people if they do not want to change. Your boss, your employees, your spouse and even your kids exclusively only change for reasons that are important to them, and never for the ones that we would like them to have. Here is a simple fact that you should never forget. The only person whose thoughts, decisions and actions you can change is looking at you in the mirror every morning. And as soon as you start changing yourself, you suddenly also change the people around you. The motto *Always go first!* applies here as well.

Self-Sabotaging-Pattern #4: Playing the victim

How you deal with setbacks, failures and problems is crucial for the sustainability of change. But how do you react when life hands you a tough test? Do you accept the challenge and decide to make the best out of the situation or do you choose to play the victim and whine about how hard things are for you? This decision determines whether you grow as a person or silently drift towards mediocrity instead.

You can either be a Changemaker or a Status Quo Manager, but never both at the same time. I want to remind you once again that you are responsible for your results in life and nobody will come to you and serve you the opportunities on a silver plate. You have to create them yourself and then take it with all you've got. If you don't do it, nobody will. But because many people aren't ready for this, they use the victim role as the perfect excuse for why they weren't able to accomplish what they set out to do a long time ago. Instead, they prefer to live in this self-created state of an emotional no man's land and get nice and cozy in their comfort zone. Growth is nearly zero. And in the long term, this creates dissatisfaction. Major dissatisfaction.

Self-Sabotaging-Pattern #5: Having an entitlement mentality

You make change happen when you take responsibility for your actions and take your fate into your own two hands. Nothing stands in the way of this attitude like the ever-growing entitlement mentality, the firm belief that one is entitled to various material things and intangible services in life and—this is the important point—without providing anything in return.

I would like to remind you of an important fact. Nothing in life is "free". If you want to get something, it has to be created first. So unleash your desire to achieve. Start creating values for other people. Give plentifully and happily. And then you should be entitled to the one thing that many people, unfortunately, seem to forget about in the confusing jungle of fictitious rights: The right to live a successful, happy and satisfied life. One that is built upon your own values, visions and dreams.

Self-Sabotaging-Pattern #6: Wanting to please everyone

How well can you say, "No"? The answer to this question is a surefire indicator of how far you have made it on your way to becoming a Changemaker. Wanting to please everyone all the time is a direct path to dissatisfaction because you distance yourself from your own personal values and principles and do things that you aren't a hundred percent sure of. The more you do something just to make your boss, your parents or your colleagues happy the less you live your own life, but follow the goals and dreams of other people instead.

Of course I don't mean that you should completely forgo helping other people, showing nice gestures and collegiality. Quite the opposite. But when it comes to your own life and your own future, you should orient yourself towards your own expectations. Wanting to make everyone happy ensures that you leave the planning of

> Don't let other people tell you how you should live you life.

your luck and your future to other people. A self-determined life assures that you go through your daily life with fun, happiness and a deep sense of satisfaction. So, learn to say no and enjoy the freedom of making decisions that rely on your core values and desires. But more about that later...

Self-Sabotaging-Pattern #7: Giving up too early

Let's get to one of most important points. There are people who implement all the aforementioned attributes and still don't reach the desired change in the end. And this happens for a simple but very decisive reason. They give up too quickly and throw in the towel as soon as the first obstacles appear in their way. But change simply does not exist without setbacks, problems and challenges. The bigger your goal is the more stones will be thrown in your way. Life will test you if you are truly serious about your change. More so, the bigger the obstacles the closer you are, most likely, to reaching your goal. You definitely have to stick it out in those cases. Changes simply need their time until they turn into a lasting habit.

Everyone Can Be a Leader

July 13th 2014 will go down in history because, on this memorable Sunday evening, multiple records were broken. Not only did the German national team win their fourth Soccer World Cup title after 1954, 1974 and 1990, but at the same time it was the first World Cup win for a European team in South America. Two days later, nearly a million people in front of the Brandenburg Gate in Berlin celebrated the team lavishly, and all of Germany was in a state of collective ecstasy.

All of Germany? Well, almost, because, even in moments of intense luck, you can find those people who are always looking for the fly in the ointment. And those who set out to find something will definitely be successful in their search. It's all a question of focus. Do you remember it from the television broadcasts? The team's happy dance, coined "Gaucho-dance" by the media, was heavily criticized because it was apparently ridiculing the losing team, which was Argentina. The fan mile in the streets of Berlin on the *Straße des 17. Juni* was way too commercialized for many of the grouches and, while they were at it, the allegedly insane salaries of the players, who are blessed with all the privileges and were born with silver spoons in their mouths, were discussed once again. Some people just manage to find a dark cloud in the most beautiful sky and only seem to be happy when they can heartily complain, whine and grumble.

> Don't let the whiners, complainers and grouches affect your attitude.

But such statements driven by envy, insecurity and resentment are usually just the outer expression of an inner fear of failing that is used to delude themselves from the mediocrity. Try your best to stay away from these kinds of people and shift your focus on to the beautiful, colorful and satisfying moments in life. They truly exist in excess. And should you feel a slight hint of envy, it's completely normal, because you are a human being after all, not a robot. What's far more important is how you deal with these feelings. A Changemaker takes delight in the success of others, and asks himself what he can learn from these people and then starts on his own way.

Mesut Özil, Toni Kroos and the other boys of Jogi Löw's (the team manager) eleven did it just like that many years ago. The president of the German Football Association, the DFB, Wolfgang Niersbach, summarized it beautifully in one of his interviews after the finale, when he said, "The world class players of today started out as regular little boys that played soccer in their village clubs. After the World Cup in 1990 they wanted to be just like Lothar Matthäus, Jürgen Klinsmann or Rudi Völler." And if you combine a big talent with a strong will and lots of hard work then a little lad named Bastian Schweinsteiger, who kicked the ball for the soccer team of *FV Oberaudorf* as a three-year-old in the pee-wee league, can become the big leader of the national team, twenty-seven years later.

If you are wondering, *Ilja, why are you writing about soccer, when this book is about change?* then please stay with me. The German national team is the perfect example of how the path of the Changemaker should look in practice. Why? Because Jogi Löw's team is full of players with a can-do attitude, who take responsibility without a title, a position or permission, and that way secure the extraordinary success of the team. Let's look at the official structure first. For years, Phillip Lahm was the captain of the team. He rose to the challenges of this position with a huge sense of responsibility and used his hierarchical title to advance the team. He was always a critical thinker, verbalized his opinion during interviews and faced the reporters' questions even after bitter defeats. And he showed true greatness when he retired from the national team immediately after the tournament, at the height of his career, to make room for the next generation.

At the same time, there were also players on the world champion team who didn't hold any title, but still acted as Changemakers, who didn't wait for permission from their coach or their captain, but actively unfolded their own personality. Next to Per Mertesacker (maybe you remember the famous "Ice ton" interview), Mats Hummels and Manuel Neuer, and especially the aforementioned Bastian Schweinsteiger, played an important role at the 2014 World Cup. Although without a captain's armband, he took responsibility during every game and carried away his teammates with his fighting spirit, commitment and will to win.

How much *Schweini* was accepted as the unofficial leader of the team became blatantly obvious during the awards ceremony after the finale. After every player went up and got their medal, it was time for the big Cup Handover. It started out pretty standard. As the highest-ranking team member, Phillip Lahm was given the trophy and held it high and proud into the evening sky of Rio de Janeiro. But it didn't take more than ten seconds for Bastian Schweinsteiger to rip the trophy from his hands and he didn't give it back again. During the following lap of honor, the obligatory photos for the gathered international press and the jubilant celebrations with the fans, it became pretty apparent to everyone who the true leader of this team was, namely Bastian Schweinsteiger. And for this standing he didn't need a title, money or permission, only his personality in combination with the attributes of a Changemaker. This is how a can-do attitude looks in practice. And it wasn't just applied by *Schweini*, but by every single player on the team, even by those who didn't spend a minute on the playing field. And that's what teamwork is all about. If every single team member works on becoming the best version of themselves and brings in their strengths as a Changemaker then the team changes as a whole and enormous successes like the win of the World Cup arise.

> Change is always about teamwork, about helping and supporting each other.

We can learn a lot from this example for our daily jobs. When it comes to leadership and successful change, many people still think they need a title, money or the necessary permission from others. The big misbelief reigns that you have to be a doctor, lawyer, CEO, department manager, boss, graduate student, director, judge, treasurer, professor or captain to actively drive change forward. And to mention this clearly once again, if you hold such a title, it is a wonderful thing because it offers you the unique opportunity to deploy all your leadership and Changemaker qualities and further develop your team.

But in the end, it always comes down to your individual personality that fills a position with life and decides if you actively develop change or prefer to passively implement the status quo. And because of this, successful change is never subject to outside factors. It never matters what is written on your business card, but what ideas, decisions and actions you use to influence your personal environment.

In every organization, every business and every team, a single individual can contribute to changes in their own sphere of influence. It really makes no difference if you are a division manager, door man or part of the facility management team. You have more opportunities than you might imagine. Every single person can be a blue-collar boss, a leader without an official position or an entrepreneur without a title. The important question is: Are you waiting for permission from others, or are you initiating changes yourself that bring you closer to your goals and dreams?

The Question That Changes Everything

If you decide not to wait any longer, but to actively implement change, you will inevitably enjoy a bunch of extraordinary experiences. You will stick out as a personality from the gray matter around you and be seen as a role model by many of your fellow humans. People will admire you for surpassing your own limits, going against the current and consequently acting according to your own values. But the more you move outside of the beaten path, the more you will be eyed critically and sometimes even treated with hostility. Just see this as a compliment of your courage and trust in your path, even if it isn't the easier of the two.

Are you still ready to make this decision? Just like in the movie *The Matrix*, you can choose between the red and the blue pill. If you choose red, everything will stay as it always has been. The cozy comfort zone and encompassing mediocrity will determine your daily life and the sentence, "We've always done it this way," becomes your mantra and permanent companion. But if you choose the blue pill, you will live life as a Changemaker and can look forward to a roller coaster ride full of ups and downs, which will rapidly lead you to more satisfaction and fulfillment in life. You will be pushed to your limits and bounce back, just to finally surpass them. But, most of all, you will learn, grow and live—in the very sense of the word. Have you made your choice?

I am a Changemaker with my whole heart and soul. There is nothing better for me than being productive, delivering value to others through my speeches, books and services, and being able to allocate my own time as I please. This is probably why I love being an entrepreneur. And the last of these three statements, in particular, almost sounds like paradise, doesn't it?

In reality, however, it's not paradise, because, as usual, everything in life has its price. Even the possibility of freely allocating your time goes along with a huge responsibility. Nobody tells me what I should or should not do. No boss follows up on my daily workflow, no colleagues are keeping me from working and no supervisors decide what is important and what is not. It all depends on me. If I'm working vigorously and am goal oriented, my customers are happy, my product quality is high and I earn decent money. But if I decide to lie in my hammock in the garden all day, this decision also has the appropriate consequences. And you know what, I love this extreme type of responsibility. This is exactly what defines the spirit of a Changemaker; to not be dependent on others, but think, decide and act independently.

This unique mindset is what connects all change-loving people. The untamed hunger for innovation. The greed for winning. The inner motivation that remains intact, even when outside factors have long changed their mind. A very special sentence helped me not only understand, but to live this mentality every day. During a trip to New York, I drove from Manhattan towards New Jersey. While driving, I passed one of the typical American billboards on which nine words that captured my gaze, almost magically, were blinking in huge letters. I don't remember what the product or who the advertising company was, but this one sentence has burned itself deeply into my mind, and has been a kind of guiding principle to me ever since. It said,

> The spirit of the Changemaker: Think, act and change according to your own values and principles.

"How hard do you play, when no one's watching?"

If you think about this question for a little while, you will realize how much dynamite is hidden behind it. The answer will tell you whether you do various things because others are expecting them of you or if you are acting out of your own inner motivation.

If you are like most people, then you complete the majority of your daily tasks because your boss is expecting them of you, because you want to look busy to your colleagues, or because it is written in your work agreement. At least in two out of these three cases, this is perfectly acceptable, because obligations are an important part of life. But would you complete these chores with the same diligence, the same intensity and the same passion if you could choose and allocate your time freely? Probably not, right? At one point or another in life, Changemakers eventually separate themselves from outside expectations and complete their tasks because they are driven by a deep inner motivation 4.0. Because they have high standards, want to offer value to other people and give meaning to their daily business.

Wonderful things start happening as soon as you start working on the spreadsheet analysis, not because your boss wants you to, but because you know that the result of your work is important for the success of the company. You not only call unhappy customers because your EDV system alerts you to the appointment, but because you are interested in solving their problems. When your inner *why* finally becomes strong enough, it leads you to making the right choices even during hard times.

No matter what challenges you are facing in the future, keep asking yourself, "How hard would I try, if nobody was watching?" Then go full throttle and start making your plans reality. Not for other people, but for yourself. OK, you might object now. "It all sounds great, Ilja, but I'm an executive in a big company (same goes for officials, teachers, employees or craftsmen). I really can't start acting like an entrepreneurial Changemaker."

But it really doesn't really matter what your actual role is. Far more important is how much emphasis you put into your work. You don't need your own business to think like an entrepreneur, because, for me, an entrepreneur is less defined by his legal status than his mindset. You can act like a Changemaker even if you are an executive, salesman or employee. Of course, the bigger the company you work in the more you have to adhere to certain guidelines.

> Take responsibility and lead the changes in your company. It doesn't matter what your actual role is.

But please don't ever use them as an excuse to fall back into your old pattern of wait-and-see. You're either thinking or acting like an entrepreneur or you just aren't. You're either actively leading as a Changemaker, or you are passively managing the status quo. You are either taking responsibility or reacting more or less randomly to the external circumstances.

I want to end this chapter with a quote by the Romanian sculptor Constantin Brancusi, which I feel is very fitting at this point. "Create like a god. Command like a king. Work like a slave." This is the exact mentality that you need to possess in order to walk along the path of the Changemaker. I wish you many beautiful experiences along the way.

Chapter Summary

Think it. Do it. Change it. The big ideas of this chapter

✓ You need a rational and an emotional reason for successful change
✓ Become a Changemaker and lead a self-determined life
✓ Take responsibility and learn to make decisions
✓ Always Go First. Put change into practice and take your co-workers, colleagues and customers along for the ride
✓ Being courageous means starting despite your fear
✓ Never place blame on anyone else. It is always you
✓ Don't wait for permission from other people, but start initiating change yourself
✓ How hard do you try when nobody is watching?

Do Not Fear Change -
Why Your Biggest Weakness Is Also Your Greatest Strength

"May the good Lord shine a light on you. Make every song you sing your favorite tune. May the good Lord shine a light on you. Warm like the evening sun."

- The Rolling Stones, Shine a Light

I love questions because they possess an incredible power. During my work as a change coach, I've often experienced that a single question can make the difference between standstill and innovation, between hesitating and acting, between frustration and a fulfilled life. But even more so, I know about the effect of strong questions that can hardly be contained out of my life. I can't remember the exact day, and I also don't remember where I was going. All I remember is that I was still a department store manager at Germany's largest retail corporation, Karstadt. What I remember is driving in my company car to attend a corporate business meeting. To distract myself from boredom, I put an audio book into the CD player of my Audi A6 and was getting ready for another trivial stream. But suddenly, without warning, the narrator asked a question that would unhinge my view on the world with a bang. "When you get up in the morning, after showering, getting dressed, eating breakfast and saying goodbye to your family, is the job you are driving to daily truly what you want to do in life?"

My first answer was impulsive. Too impulsive. It was, after all, my dream job, for which I had studied many years, worked hard and sacrificed a lot in my private life. But I was seized by the question and it started to rattle inside my head. And while time and space blurred around me, a new, deeply honest answer started to make its way to the surface. Combined with the realization that became more and more apparent, I suddenly felt a feeling I hadn't felt in this intensity before. I was afraid. Terribly afraid. Afraid of the truth.

Only years later I realized that this was an important turning point in my life. Because nothing affects our decisions as much as fear does. It can hinder us, make us hesitate and paralyze us. On the other hand, it can also be a huge driving force, motivator and pioneer. Despite it all, the subject of fear still remains a taboo in our society. We fear nothing more than honestly admitting that we are afraid.

And yet fear rules the life of every single person on this planet. There are no exceptions. And if you should run into one of the usual suspects again, that want to tell you that they aren't afraid, then you can be sure that they are lying to you. Everyone is afraid. Just like you are. The tenured teacher and the smart multimillionaire. Small children and old, wise men. The caring housewife and the CEO of a fortune 500 company. The seventeen-year-old apprentice and the pope. We are all driven by fear. It is the main reason why we do certain things and not others. Care for a few examples?

- We don't change out of fear of the unknown
- We take on insurance policies because of fear of a loss
- Out of fear of getting older, we go under the knife at the plastic surgeon's office and inject Botox into our lips
- Out of fear of not belonging, we buy cars, clothes and electronics that we really can't afford in the first place
- We don't speak out about what's important to us, because we are afraid of offending someone
- We complete our daily routines at work merely for the reason that we are afraid of being fired
- We hole up behind huge fences out of fear of burglaries
- Out of fear of rejection, we wear uncomfortable masks and play roles that don't fit us at all
- Out of fear of getting fat, we start running or sign up at the gym
- Out of fear of losing security, we don't dare to exercise the freedom we dream of

THINK IT. DO IT. CHANGE IT.

- Out of fear of dying we miss out on truly living
- Out of fear of not finding anything better, we make the daily drive to a job that frustrates us, makes us unhappy or that we even hate

What else can you think of? I could have gone on forever with this list. But I think the point was made clear, am I right? A little while ago, I watched the movie *Eat.Pray.Love* with Julia Roberts in the starring role again. And one sentence really stuck with me, as it gets to the heart of this entire list in a precisely tragic way: "We deal with being unhappy out of fear of changes, out of fear everything could collapse."

> Embrace your fears. When you are able to turn them into productive energy, you have the most powerful ally by your side.

Whether we like it or not, fear is the deciding factor when it comes to change. Either we accomplish things because we are afraid of not doing them or we don't do things because we are afraid of doing them. A life without fear does not exist, and the sooner you accept this fact the better you will deal with it. Because it is so important, I would like to emphasize two things:

1. It is perfectly normal to be afraid.
2. How we deal with our fear determines our level of happiness, success and our general quality of life.

We are going to deal especially with the second statement in detail in this chapter. How do you accomplish taking your fear by the horns? How can you make your fear a strong ally that drives you to use your full potential? How do you use your fear to implement changes that you never thought were possible to achieve? As soon as you find the right answer to these questions, you own the key to a kingdom named Change. Because when you are able to turn your fear into productive energy, you have the most powerful ally possible by your side.

The Fear is Your Friend

I'm a huge fan of good blockbuster movies. I especially love the Batman series with Christian Bale in the leading role. The last part of this trilogy is called *The Dark Knight Rises*, and the turning point of this story occurs in an abandoned prison where his opponent, Bane, locks up Bruce Wayne—a.k.a. Batman. Hundreds of meters below the surface, there is only a steep shaft that offers a possible escape route to freedom. Many prisoners before him have attempted to escape the horror this way. With only a rope for safety, they carefully climbed to the top foot by foot. But nobody ever succeeded in escaping. Some got lucky and injured themselves badly enough, but most of them died.

After a few weeks in the dungeon, Bruce Wayne dared to try an escape attempt but he failed repeatedly, and the crucial jump over the crevice just wouldn't work out—until he received a tip from his wise cellmate one day. He said, "Do you want to know the reason why you aren't succeeding? It's your fear."

"No, I'm not afraid. I'm angry", Bruce replied.

To which the old man countered, "But how can you be extraordinarily fast, extraordinarily strong and fight extraordinarily long, if you can't rely on the biggest strength possible? The fear of death." These words went straight to his heart and Batman gave it another try, but this time without the presumed securing rope. And his fear gave him unimagined strength; so he did finally succeed in climbing up the shaft, escaping into freedom and saving Gotham City from destruction.

Of course, this scene is brought to the screen in typical Hollywood manner, with emotional music and just the right amount of pathos. But the message is far from being diminished: Fear is our best friend, if we allow it to be. But at the same time, that is the big challenge that keeps so many people from approaching necessary changes and making their dreams come true. Instead of seeing fear as a powerful ally, they let themselves be dominated, hindered or paralyzed by it. And then they find themselves in a negative spiral that's only getting stronger, and is very hard to escape. The results are fatal, because the fears we don't face become our limits. The doubts we give into turn into walls that make these limits even stronger and harder to overcome.

"But Ilja," you might object now, "that's easier said than done, because really successful people probably don't know anything about fear anyway."

> Fear is your best friend, if you allow it to be.

Far from it. I am even going to allege that the intensity of your fears rises proportionally as your dreams grow, your undertakings become more absurd and your changes get more courageous. No, let me emphasize it one more time: Every human being has fears. The crucial question, solely and exclusively, is how you deal with them; whether you let yourself be paralyzed by your inner demons, or if you make fear your best friend. And to help you accomplish exactly that, I would like to introduce my four most effective fear busters to you.

Fear-Buster #1: Accept that it is okay to be afraid

Please do not ever buy in to the misbelief that being afraid is a sign of weakness. Quite the opposite. Have I mentioned that everyone is afraid? Good, so I hope we have cleared this up once and for all and can move on to the next step. Because if it is perfectly normal to you to have these feelings then you are well on your way to turning this alleged weakness into a huge strength. The more offensively you deal with your fears the more you are able to face them actively, tackle them and, in the end, overcome them. This quickly turns into a positive spiral that strengthens itself. Every defeated fear helps you to learn, grow as a person and get stronger.

Fear-Buster #2: Be consciously aware of your motivation

Can you remember a situation where you changed only after the psychological strain got unbearable? Most likely you've hesitated in taking the important first step multiple times, because your fear of change (of the unknown) was much bigger than all the negative things that bothered you about the status quo. The reasoning for this usually goes something like this, "Who knows if it's not going to get even worse?" Heard that before? Said that before?

People with a can-do attitude simply turn the tables. Instead of fearing the unknown things in the future, they are much more afraid that everything might stay as it is. And this fear drives them. It pushes them into taking action more than any goal in the world ever could. I'm even going to claim that fear is the biggest motivator that anyone can have. It supplies you with the maximum amount of adrenaline, discipline and endurance. The only question is whether you use these enormous resources to hide inside of your bunker or if you spring into action and use this fear productively for change.

Fear-Buster #3: Control the movie inside your head

Most changes are great. Unfortunately, we don't find out about this until we have made them. Beforehand, the movie inside our head keeps playing. In our mind we imagine, in the most vibrant colors, all the things that could go wrong, how bad the consequences will be and why we definitely shouldn't change anything. The process is almost always the same. We have an important task to accomplish and, in theory, we know exactly what we have to do. But then we hesitate and say things like, "I'm just not ready, I'm too old, I'm too young, it's too early, this is happening too fast, it's happening too slow, I'm definitely not going to be able to do it."

Sounds familiar, doesn't it? The more you keep telling yourself these things the more these excuses turn into a self-fulfilling prophecy, fear increases, and you miss out on taking that crucial first step. Muster up all your courage in these situations and face your inner conflicts. Many concerns simply dissolve themselves while you are acting.

Nobody knows this as well as Jack Ma. This five ft. small Chinese man, who is considered the Asian Bill Gates, put the biggest public offering in history behind him in 2015 and is a multibillionaire today. But it wasn't always like this. Ma grew up poor and failed his entrance exam at the university twice before he saw his first computer in the 90s. And when he got connected to the Internet during this special moment, he felt deep inside of him that this was an invention that would change the world. So he quit his job as an English teacher, borrowed money from his friends and opened the online shop *Alibaba.com* in 1999, without any economical or technical knowledge, right in his own living room.

Today his company has 25,000 employees and over 300 million customers worldwide. Recently, Jack Ma was giving a speech in front of Stanford graduates and revealed his secret of success to the students. "Dare to do something in life. Work hard and take a risk. Nothing bad can possibly happen."

And right he is. Whenever you are facing a change in the future, whenever you feel doubt, insecurity or fear, I recommend you ask yourself these two questions:

1. What is the worst thing that could happen?
2. If the worst should happen, am I able to find a solution for it?

And you usually can, because reality is never as bad as the movie in our head would like us to believe sometimes. Even in the absolute worst-case scenario, you are able to find a solution. I would like to give you an example. When I made the decision to open up my own business, I was very afraid of the crucial first step because the status quo was just too comfortable. I had a secure corporate job, was making great money, drove a swanky company car and various career doors were wide open to me. And I was supposed to give up all this? For something that I didn't even know was going to work out? Believe me, the movie in my head was running wild and painted me a colorful picture of how badly I would fail.

But, eventually, I stopped running away from my fear and asked myself, "What is the worst thing that could happen?" The answer came to me fast: I was going to fail ceremoniously; my business would go bankrupt and turn out to be nothing but a pipe dream. This was the worst thing that could happen.

> Use the four fear-busters to transform your fears into a powerful force of change.

Based on this, I asked myself, "If this worst-case scenario happens, will I be able to find a solution?" This answer gave me additional strength and a comforting knowledge. No matter what happened, I knew I was not going to die and my family was still going to love me. I had friends whose support I could count on at any time. And I was qualified enough to be sure that I would always find another good job. What once was fear had suddenly turned into a courage that could hardly be contained, so I said to myself, *I'm just going to do it!*

Fear-Buster #4: Start taking action

After shifting your focus on to possible solutions, it is time to make the first step because fears start to disappear as soon as we start facing them. And once we have overcome them, they make us stronger, more hopeful and courageous. Whenever you feel doubt, insecurity and fear, you should always promise yourself to take any kind of action. As small as a single step may seem, every one of them brings you a bit closer to your final goal.

Imagine you are walking through a dark forest and the only thing you are carrying with you is a small flashlight. Your visibility is limited to three feet due to the small beam, so you only walk as far as you can see. Then you shine the flashlight again and continue on your way. And then you shine again and keep walking. This way you pass through the unknown terrain step by step until you eventually reach your goal.

I truly hope that these four steps will be a faithful companion in transforming your fears into productive emotions. If fear is your biggest enemy then you are facing a fight that you cannot win. Remind yourself of the following idea as often as possible: The fears that we do not face will turn into our limits. The doubts that we give in to turn into walls that will make these limits stronger and harder to overcome. I want to encourage you to tear these walls down and overcome your mental limits. And as soon as fear becomes your loyal ally, you will experience a wonderful feeling of freedom. But, most of all, you unleash an inner strength, with which you are able to accomplish the most unbelievable things.

Change with a Purpose

There is hardly an area in life where fear dominates our way of acting as much as in business. This has a simple reason behind it, because nowhere else do two of the most important human values clash in such a violent fashion. I'm talking about security on one hand and the need for freedom on the other. Recently, I read a study while on a plane that stated that new employees already know after about two weeks whether they will remain with a company for the long term. And still the average person doesn't quit until two years later, due to unhappiness. Conversely, it's similar. The companies usually know after about three to six months whether they want to keep a new employee. But even if the answer to this question is no, they usually don't fire him until an average of three years. The reason for this irrational behavior? Plain and simple, fear. Fear of not finding a better job. Fear of not finding a better employee. Fear of a possible conflict. And so we would rather deal with the alternative, which leads inevitably to one condition: Discontent.

I experienced myself, a couple of years ago, what consequences such triggered behavior can have when I gave a speech about employee motivation to a well-known retail company. Actually, everything went as it always did, until I got a call from my speakers' bureau a few days later. Because the audience was very enthusiastic after the speech, I was looking forward to positive feedback from the customer. But I was mistaken; instead I received a complaint, because two branch managers quit their jobs the very same day. The fingers were pointed at me because I spoke about the meaning of your own work, the power of motivation 4.0 and active change during my speech. And I admit this accusation ate away at me back then because I was pondering about if and how I could have prevented it.

What helped me was a conversation with an entrepreneur that I was friends with, who told me the following: "What kind of company is this that's afraid that their employees are going to run away, as soon as the focus shifts to company values and conditions? Personally, I would be more scared that they will stay, even though they mentally quit a long time ago." Right he was. Way too many compromises are being made by employees, as well as by the companies. You've probably heard about the famous Gallup study, right? It is now being used as almost inflationary material by speakers, writers and performers of every color, and it states the following: Only fourteen percent of all employees had strong ties to their companies in 2014. Instead, sixty-one percent felt very weak ties, and a whole twenty-three percent had mentally quit already and were only physically present (and not even that at times, hello doctor's note!).

Find a job that challenges you, satisfies you and that you are grateful for.

These circumstances always break my heart, because such an unhappiness driven by fear should not even exist. Because we spend the majority of our waking state at work, nothing should be of higher priority than working in a job that challenges us, satisfies us and that we are grateful for. And companies of any size should also make a conscious effort to make their employees feel welcome and help them reach their full potential. Visionary entrepreneurs have long realized this fact. If people can introduce their abilities, talents and strengths into the right work environment, then they are able to offer extraordinary contributions.

Richard Branson—multibillionaire, owner of over 260 companies and founder of the Virgin group—summarized it on his blog very fittingly with the following sentence: "Give your employees a mission that meets their needs. If you challenge people you will be surprised what they are capable of." I know a lot of companies that have understood this connection and invest a lot of energy, time and money into creating a lasting company culture that's characterized by strong values. Ask an employee at Zappos, IKEA or Jack & Jones if they know a colleague that has mentally quit. I can predict that you will get many quizzical looks.

Of course, there are also plenty of companies that don't place much importance on making employee retention a higher priority. Maybe you even work in one of these companies. It would be the easiest thing in the world to join the choir of whiners and complain about how horrible your own job is, but I would like to remind you, at this point, how much power personal responsibility can have. If you should feel the slightest inkling of unhappiness at work, I would like to invite you to promise yourself to actively change something about it, right here and right now. What do I mean by this? I'm talking about the responsibility to yourself to turn your boring and frustrating profession into a meaningful occupation that you complete daily with high motivation, not just once, but every single day.

Remember: A job is only an ordinary job if you decide to value it as such. Instead, nearly every occupation imaginable offers you the opportunity to express your unique talents and skills. But this is only possible if what you do eight (or more in many cases) hours a day has a deeper meaning and fills you with satisfaction in the morning and gratitude in the evening. So, let us take a look at three possibilities to use the power of a useful occupation to considerably increase the degree of personal responsibility, success and satisfaction. Nothing stifles the feeling of fear like purpose-driven thinking and acting, because suddenly you start to act out of a state of certainty that supplies you with a huge amount of courage and determination.

> A job is only an ordinary job if you decide to value it as such.

Meaningful factor #1: Notice the existing meaning

I keep noticing how much of a knee-jerk reaction people have to things at their place of employment that they cannot influence anyway. The unfair supervisor, the lazy colleagues and the way-too-demanding customers bother them. They complain about conditions, company politics and wish back the good old times. While doing that, they forget to look on the bright side of things, at what's working fine and what makes their own place of employment something special.

I am wholly convinced that truly every job can have its good sides and a deeper meaning—yes, truly every one—but only if you are willing to notice them. So have a close look. Look at the values of your company, the parts that you love about your job and the many little things that fill your heart with joy as soon as you think about them. With such a focus, your ordinary job will turn into a meaningful occupation shaped by satisfaction that offers you the change to express your own greatness.

Meaningful factor #2: Create your own meaning

If, after a thorough search, you absolutely cannot find anything meaningful about your current job, please stifle the impulse of taking on the role of the victim. Start getting active instead. I recently read a nice quote on Instagram: "The world is full of wonderful people. If you can't find one, be one." This has a point, doesn't it? And the same goes for the question about the meaning of our job.

Even your company, your working place and your job description are full of meaningful aspects. And if you cannot find one, you will just have to create some yourself. There are countless opportunities to give meaning to seemingly unimportant things—accounting, telephone conversations with customers, conversations with co-workers or on the subway ride to your company.

"But, Ilja, what kind of meaning could these things even have?" I can think of a few possibilities; for example, because it is important to a specific customer, because you are contributing something to the team, because your industry serves an important social purpose or because you want to be a role model to your colleagues. And sometimes the biggest meaning simply lies in a single aspect: What you do is the right thing to do. Because you signed a contract, you said you were going to do it or because someone is relying on you.

Meaningful factor #3: Stop doing things that have no meaning

I can guarantee that you can turn your ordinary job into a meaningful profession with these two options in over ninety-five percent of all cases. But what if you cannot manage to find or create even a little spark of meaning in your job, no matter how hard you try? Then you should try to find a meaningful alternative as soon as possible and follow the notorious wisdom of change: Love it, change it or leave it.

The thought alone scares you? But what is the alternative, that you keep doing things that frustrate you, restrict you and make you unhappy for eight hours a day? That brings it to forty hours a week, 160 a month and 1,920 a year that you are spending at a job that you don't like, despise or even hate. Shouldn't this fact scare you a whole lot more? Face this fear, tear down the mental walls and create a living and working environment that has meaning. You will not regret it.

> Always follow the old wisdom: "Love it, change it or leave it."

The Only Fear you Should Have

Franklin Delano Roosevelt spoke a sentence in his first speech as the President of the United States of America during his inauguration on March 4th, 1933 that is still one of the most famous quotes in history, "The only thing we should fear is fear itself." Sounds pretty logical, right? But I am convinced that exactly the opposite is the case. By now, this idea that every person has fears has hopefully moved into your head. Some of them are small, some bigger. But we all have them, even Bruce Springsteen, Tiger Woods or Barack Obama. No matter what great person we admire for their unique actions, they all have to fight the same doubts, insecurities and fears as you and I. And this is for a simple reason. A life without fear simply does not exist. Fear of the unknown is a normal result of daring to make a change, making courageous decisions or striking out in a new direction.

Having no fear would inevitably mean that you are living a life of mediocrity, comfort and standstill. That we don't dare to take a risk, but rather play it safe. That we have stopped growing as a person, stopped evolving and lead a miserable existence in a mental no man's land. And I don't know about you, but the thought alone gives me goose bumps.

No, if this was the price I had to pay to live a life without fear then I am happy for every little bit of doubt, every insecurity and every single fear. Because these feelings not only show me that I am alive, but that I am well on my way of doing something that will make me grow as a person. After all, the biggest breakthroughs always lie in the changes that we fear the most.

Therefore, I am firmly convinced that there is only one fear we should have—the fear of not being afraid anymore. I even dare to claim that the degree of fear is a good indicator of how big our dreams truly are. If you don't feel a bit of doubt and fear during a change, you can be sure that your endeavor is not nearly challenging enough. And another thing is important. Most fears turn out to be unfounded in hindsight. It is the movie in our head that constantly supplies us with detailed horror scenarios that makes us hesitate and wait. But once we successfully face that fear, we also constantly realize that reality isn't quite as bad as the images in our head have made us believe. Fear is an illusion.

And believe me, I know what I'm talking about. For years, it was one of my biggest fears to have a blackout on stage during one of my speeches. I colorfully imagined all the horrible things that would happen if this mental picture became reality. And one day I accomplished it. My own personal horror scenarios had turned into a self-fulfilling prophecy.

> The only fear you should have is not to be afraid anymore.

I was standing on a big stage. Bright spotlights were shining down on me and three hundred people were sitting in front of me. Up to this point, everything was running fine. I was completely in my element, the audience was laughing a lot and the spark was catching more and more as the minutes passed. I just finished an inspiring story about bungee jumping and the audience was clapping enthusiastically. Enjoying the experience, I allowed myself to be carried away by the moment and was just about to get to the next point when, suddenly, something happened. Exactly nothing. From one moment to the next my mind was completely wiped clean; I was at a loss for words and had completely lost my train of thought. What I feared the most suddenly became reality. I experienced a classic blackout and was desperately searching for an opportunity to curl up and die out of shame, while thee hundred pairs of eyes were looking at me expectantly.

And I don't know where the impulse came from, but for some reason I remembered what I always reiterate in my books and speeches, namely that it is better to do something instead of freezing. So I started acting and slowly moved towards the speakers' desk where my MacBook Air was located. There I took deep breath and had a sip of water, and, suddenly, without any prior warning, everything came back to me—my words, my train of thought and also my confidence. I walked back to the middle of the stage and just continued talking.

Isn't real life the best teacher? What we fear the most isn't as bad as we expect it to be most of the time. Quite the opposite. If you offensively deal with your fears you can turn any kind of challenge into something positive in the end. Actually, the audience hadn't even noticed that I had a blackout. The whole drama played out exclusively in my own head.

There was huge applause after my talk and everyone was satisfied. And the cherry on top was a remark from a lady in the third row, who approached me with a smile and said, "Mr. Grzeskowitz, this was great, you really spoke to my heart. And do you know what I liked the most? That pause you made after your story about bungee jumping, when you slowly walked to your desk. It really gave me time to think about my own changes."

Intention Beats Everything

If you dare to overcome the doubts, insecurities and fears of your daily life then you live a life at the edge of your comfort zone. But such a place, not known to many people, can be quite lonely, because the majority would rather take the easy way out, and concentrate on the well-known convenience of what is known as normal. By doings this, they keep narrowing their mental and physical abilities more and more, which are being fearfully guarded by tall walls. But just like the Irish playwright George Bernhard Shaw once said, "What we need is a few crazy people. Look where the normal people have taken us." Therefore, I would like to invite you to be one of these positively mad people. To think crazy, act courageously and live a fulfilled life.

Last week, I noticed once again how much the world is waiting for people just like you when I read an article about the company Google during my research. There, it is an official rule to think crazy and passionately. If this wasn't the case, the creativity and productivity would not be kept on the same level, according to the manager interviewed. So, how crazy have you already thought today? What makes your heart beat a little bit faster? Whatever it is for you, you should definitely be doing these things more often. Dare to think crazy. Exceedingly few passions can be explained rationally and on the edge of the comfort zone is where all the magic happens!

Your daily life suddenly becomes more colorful, intense and fulfilled if you do things that you've never done before, make courageous decisions and have invaluable experiences that immediately let you grow as a person. And I don't mean you should spend your days bungee jumping, extreme climbing or skydiving from now on. No, your true comfort zone is defined by the sum of all the seemingly small situations of everyday life; the constantly pushed off complaint of a customer, the difficult decision at work, the unpleasant call to your boss or the courageous acting when everyone else is hesitating.

I know that this doesn't sound very appealing, but these are the moments that separate the wheat from the chaff, the moments in which everyday heroes are born. In addition, the more you overcome your fears through change, the more you will push the limits of your comfort zone. And before you know it, you inevitably set off an invisible positive spiral. Your decisions become more courageous, your actions more confident and your previous weakness turns into your biggest strength.

> Make a conscious effort to expand the limits of your comfort zone.

I am aware that this sounds a lot easier on paper than it is to implement into daily life. But there is a factor that can be a loyal companion to you on this rocky road. And maybe this will surprise you, but I am not talking about technology, not about a method and also not about a certain process. The key that will open all the doors to success in your life is your own intention.

It doesn't matter if you communicate with your co-workers, are faced with a complicated negotiation, or want to teach your children an important lesson. Your results rise and fall with the expectations you place in the small and large tasks of everyday life, because intention beats everything. Others might be smarter, faster or more talented than you, but if you approach your task with the right intention, you will always be that famous step ahead of the competition.

But what exactly do I mean when I say intention? To me, it's the mentality with which you accomplish things. A clear expectation of the end result of the upcoming communications. The absence of doubts, and the deep certainty that you will achieve exactly what you set out to do. This applies to sales discussions, conflicts and negotiations, as well as flirting, conversations with your relatives and raising your children.

Your concrete expectations might vary, depending on the situation, but there is one aspect you should always apply from now on. Enter every single communication with the intention that your counterpart will be better off after the encounter. This way, you open Pandora's Box, which has unexpected treasures waiting for you inside.

And this brings us to another important factor of intention, why and how you are communicating with other people. Are you surprised by what you say, because you are rather spontaneous? Do you sometimes just exchange some empty phrases because it's expected in certain situations? Then I would like to make the following idea attractive to you. Stop entering conversations, discussions or other forms of communication without having a specific goal in mind. Start thinking about what exactly you want your counterparts to think, do and especially how they should feel afterwards. The clearer you are in your expectations about which goal you are trying to attain the better action you can take. You will be surprised how fast people can feel that you are acting out of the right intentions. The more you shift your focus to the outside, to your customers, co-workers and family members the faster you will also reach your own goals. Everything in life truly revolves around your relationships with other people.

Here's an example. Last year we spent our family vacation in Florida, where we had breakfast at Denny's in Fort Lauderdale one morning. As soon as we sat down in our booth, the waiter came over. His name was Bobby and he started joking right away as he introduced himself. Then he brought us the menus and asked, "Hey, are you ready for the best French toast in town?" He definitely had my attention.

And Bobby continued with his high standards. He had two small gifts for our kids in his pocket and he gave my wife a coupon that we could use to save on dinner that day. Then he asked what we were doing in his hometown, told us about his time in the Army in Germany and kept making us laugh. Soon we found a common passion and started talking about golf, tennis and all the other recreational opportunities in the area. Bobby was never pushy, but managed to make us completely comfortable in no time at all. After we were done eating, he offered to save us the best seat in the restaurant for the next day.

Where do you think we ate 24 hours later? More so, even though this Denny's wasn't quite around the corner from our hotel, and I'm sure there would have been better choices available, we had breakfast at this restaurant daily until our departure. Not because of the amazing food, it was ok, but nothing more, and not because of the good prices or the not-so-special atmosphere; we chose this restaurant strictly because of Bobby, who managed to build a meaningful relationship during our first meeting. This made us feel comfortable and after almost a week we felt a little bit at home at the Denny's in Fort Lauderdale. Of course, we also spent a good amount of money for our food and Bobby's tip was more than lavish as well.

Because I was so fascinated by our loyalty to this mediocre-at-best restaurant, I asked him during our final goodbye how he manages to still be so friendly and courteous despite the monotone process as a waiter. He laughed for a moment and then he said, "Well, that's easy, I just like people."

> Enter every single communication with the intention that your counterpart will be better off after the encounter.

"I just like people." This sentence summarizes the effect of intentional conversations perfectly. It's always about people. If you manage to make a personal connection with your co-workers, colleagues and customers, the greatest things will happen. When people feel comfortable they will act accordingly. Your revenue, negotiation successes and all results of your communications are directly connected to the intensity of the relationships you build with other people.

And another exciting thing will happen. You will be able to deal with the fear of change much better, because nothing is quite as powerful as the right intention. You are no longer acting randomly, arbitrarily and trivially, but start to give a specific meaning to every single moment in your life. This applies to the small problems, but especially to the big challenges.

The power of intention

- Intention brings clarity
- Intention strengthens your self-esteem
- Intention eliminates doubt

- Intention forms an invisible band between two people
- Intention offers certainty
- Intention creates positive feelings
- Intention replaces arbitrariness with meaning
- Intention creates the right focus
- Intention motivates
- Intention is more important than all techniques, methods and processes combined
- Intention beats everything

Whenever you are a bit afraid to do something, you should deliberately use your intention. Your expectation can be your ass in the sleeve that holds the balance between success and misfortune. The best thing about it is that you will be completely separated from external factors because your intention is something that you can control from start to finish. The better you are at this the more confident, convinced and successful you will be in these moments, and therefore be able to enjoy the inevitably following roller coaster ride.

This doesn't mean everything is suddenly going to run smoothly just like magic; that you won't make any more mistakes and there won't be any moments where things go wrong. Quite the opposite, the chances are good that this will happen to you frequently, because those who make a lot of decisions happen to be wrong sometimes. But if you are acting intentionally you will never regret your failures, because you know that you are in the process of overcoming your fears, learning from your mistakes and growing as a person.

Now I'd like to ask you an important question, my dear readers. How comfortable are you at the edge of your comfort zone? How do you deal with doubt, insecurity and fear? How about your intention? If you look around, you will realize how many people wear various masks in their roles as bosses, co-workers, colleagues, friends, spouses or neighbors, in order to disguise their true personality. Don't you know people in your social circle who function almost robot like during their daily jobs, who communicate awkwardly and let themselves be put into an existing mold? Then they completely lighten up when they get home in the evenings, where they play with their kids in the yard, laugh with their friends and finally do what's important to them.

Let's not fool ourselves; all of us wear these kinds of masks, sometimes more, sometimes less. Most of them we have picked out ourselves, because we believe that we have to oblige to certain expectations or presumed rules. But the more comfortable these chosen masks are, the further we distance ourselves from our inner core. The reason, plain and simple, is fear—fear of having to explain yourself, being rejected or simply being yourself.

How do you manage to face these fears and even overcome them? The solution lies in the root of your intentions. To get closer to this, I would like to ask you two questions that have the potential to really get down to business. In order to answer them, you have to face your fears and get in touch with your true desires, your inner conflicts and your deepest aspirations. These exact things make up your intentions. Are you ready for this? Here are the two questions. You're familiar with the first one. It's the question that shook up my view on the world a few years ago:

When you get up in the morning, after showering, getting dressed, eating breakfast and saying goodbye to your family, is the job you are driving to daily truly what you want to do in life?

Are you already breaking a sweat? Here is question number two:

When you get home at night, after a hard eight hours of work, and put your key into the door, exhausted, is this the place with exactly the people you would love to be with right now?"

> Intention beats everything. So find out what's important to you.

It's always fascinating to me how powerful these two questions are. I ask them often during my seminars and over the years I've made a fascinating discovery. About one third of those asked answer both questions with a clear *Yes*, and a bit more than half at least one of the two. I've asked myself for a long time why this number is so low, but today I am sure that the reason is that many people simply lead a life that puts their own desires in the background and is guided towards the expectations of others, because they are afraid of taking the deciding step and the possibly uncontrollable consequences.

How did you feel answering these questions? Were you able to answer with a resounding *Yes*, or did you feel a little bit of fear? Either way, you can be happy because by now you should know how to handle both alternatives. Fight for your dreams, but never against yourself.

The more you dare to express your inner desires through your ideas, words and actions the more meaning you put into your job, your business and your life because you are suddenly acting with goal oriented intentions, because you communicate what you think, feel and want to achieve in verbal as well as nonverbal ways. Then it's time to take the next step and start on the path to creating the best version of yourself. We will take a closer look at how this is best done and what exactly it entails in the next chapter.

Chapter Summary

Think it. Do it. Change it. The big ideas of this chapter

- ✓ Fear is the deciding driver when it comes to changes
- ✓ Everyone, without exception, is afraid
- ✓ The fears we do not face turn into our limitations
- ✓ Accept that it is OK to be afraid
- ✓ Ask yourself: "What is the worst thing that could happen?" and just start
- ✓ Promise yourself to take action every time you are afraid
- ✓ A job is only ordinary if you decide to value it as such
- ✓ The only fear you should have is of not being afraid anymore
- ✓ Dare to think crazy and lead a life at the edge of your comfort zone
- ✓ The right intention beats everything and is more important than all techniques, methods and processes combined
- ✓ Fight for your dreams but never against yourself

Use Your Uniqueness -
Why It Pays to Be Awesome

"When I was just a baby my mama told me: Son, always be a good boy, don't ever play with guns. But I shot a man in Reno just to watch him die. When I hear that whistle blowin', I hang my head and cry."
- Johnny Cash, Folsom Prison Blues

"Men wanted for hazardous journey. Low wages, bitter cold, long hours of complete darkness. Safe return doubtful. Honor and recognition in event of success." With this advertisement, the British polar explorer Sir Ernest Shackleton was searching for courageous comrades-in-arms for his planned Antarctica expedition in the year 1914. And it doesn't quite sound like the typical job advertisement a modern human resource manager would write today, does it? Who is willingly going to take such a risk? Who would willingly endure the bitter cold, months of darkness and the minimal chance of a safe return? But you'd be surprised, because for over five thousand men and three women these prospects seemed to be the biggest motivation when they applied for this expedition. Fifty-six of them set sail with Sir Ernest Shackleton on board the arctic vessel *Endurance*, heading towards the South pole.

What about you, would you have applied to this ad? I'm asking because, in this chapter, I would like to get you excited about an expedition that needs just as much boldness, courage and daring as the expedition into the eternal ice did exactly a hundred years ago. I'm talking about the way to individual uniqueness, the courage of living your own values and making your biggest dreams reality. The journey of being awesome. And I'm definitely not talking about the trend that's currently running rampant—"The most important thing is to be different"—which seems to have become an all-dominant mantra for an entire generation.

Is this not the case? Everyone wants to be different nowadays, at all costs, come what may. The reasons don't always matter, the most important thing is to be different. This "I'm-completely-different" mentality is usually reflected in outfits, attitudes and, when it comes to companies, by having the most diverse marketing channels. But the interesting question is why so many people feel almost compelled to be different. I think it's the desire of the masses to finally not be a part of the masses anymore. And this desire turns into a search for easily implementable ways to set themselves apart from it.

Despite it all, I have the feeling that the majority isn't very happy with the results of this philosophy. The more you desperately try to be different the more you distance yourself from your own identity. You live according to the values and ideas of other people, and while doing this forget what's important to you. But, to me, the biggest irony is this: If we are all different suddenly then we are all the same in the end, right? This is why I would like to invite you to think about a much more daring idea.

> Don't do what society expects you to do. Be awesome instead.

Instead of following a fake "being different at any cost"(and looking to the outside) mentality, it's worth taking a look at your unique personality (on the inside). Only when you allow yourself to let your own unique character show do you take the deciding step to differentiate yourself from the masses. And to be unique happens to be something completely different than just being different. Your values, beliefs, talents, abilities, your knowledge and your very own identity all make up your own unique personality, if you dare to perceive them and live them outwardly. And suddenly you will be different, but in a way that's unique to the world. Awesome.

Extraordinary Instead of Ordinary

It has never been easier than it is today to stand out from the masses and make a difference. Wherever you look, you will notice one domineering circumstance: Mediocrity. Most jobs are mediocre, the quality of most products and services is mediocre, and most of the customer service is usually mediocre as well. The masses aren't really satisfied, but they're not completely dissatisfied either.

Yesterday, while waiting at the airport, I observed a conversation between two businessmen that I find typical for this kind of lifestyle. One of the gentlemen asked his colleague, "So, how's it going?"

The other man sighed and answered, "Well, it's going. And you?"

To which his conversation partner shrugged his shoulders and said, "Same here. You just fight your way through it."

I'm sure you've experienced a conversation like that before, right? The attitude towards life in today's affluent society can be described pretty accurately with "so-so". Just mediocre. And because mediocrity is so ever-present, the life plans of most people tend to drift in this direction as well. The long-term job, the relationship with your spouse and your kids, as well as the general feeling of satisfaction eventually level off and are neither fish nor fowl. Instead of actively changing all these things, you'd rather deal with the mediocrity and manage the unloved status quo—because who knows if it is not going to get worse?

Time to change this, don't you think? Marketing guru Seth Godin, who I value highly, said two very remarkable things in his book *Purple Cow*. For one, he determined that the supposedly safe ways in times of ever-expanding change have become the new risk. Furthermore, he says, you can either be invisible or extraordinary as a person.

In my opinion, he hit the nail right on the head. If you turn around the first one of Godin's determinations, you have a really good strategy. Consciously taking risks has long become the only safe path. Acting instead of waiting is the motto that you need to keep envisioning daily. I am firmly convinced that you can only be successful in the present time if you leave the beaten paths and dare to actively initiate necessary changes and make risky decisions sometimes. When you bid your excuses goodbye, and take on responsibility instead. When you stop waiting and start on the path to your individual unique personality. Believe me, in a world where mediocrity reigns supreme, you will stand out in no time at all.

> Say goodbye to mediocrity and dare to make risky decisions.

The biggest risk today is taking the supposedly safe path, relying on concepts that have long become obsolete and giving in to the hope that everything is going to be okay. Danish physicist Niels Bohr once said, "Predictions are difficult, especially if they have to do with the future." Nevertheless, I am daring to make one. In the next ten years we will be confronted with changes that will have drastic effects on society, the business world and our everyday life. What was the standard yesterday can already be outdated today and change again tomorrow. The markets are dramatically reinventing themselves and the customers are behaving completely different than they did just a few years ago.

Reports about currency crises, civil wars and recessions have become a normal part of everyday life as well. Major companies go bankrupt and a huge amount of today's jobs won't exist anymore in the near future. Everything is changing; nothing stays the same. However, even during times of rapid change, there is a constant, a fixed point and a hub that you can align your life plans with at any time, with confidence.

I'm talking about you. You as a person. Your uniqueness. You alone are the only factor you can really rely on. Jobs, crises, companies, trends and changes come and go, but you will always be there, and the more solidified your individual identity is the easier it will be to weather bigger storms, head winds and challenges. Therefore, you should invest in your own individual uniqueness as much and as often as possible, in your knowledge, your abilities and your personal development. The risk has long become the new safe.

For that, it's crucial that you set out on your way. Your own way. Not one that others have chosen for you, but one that brings you closer to your goals, your expectations and your dreams. It doesn't matter where you are today, what business you are currently in, what starting point you are at, or how good you already are today.

I've worked with hundreds of entrepreneurs and executives in the past fifteen years, the young and the old, the good, the bad and the ugly, the motivated and the disillusioned ones. In the sum of these experiences I have noticed one thing; it's never about being the best at everything. Much less is it about comparing yourself with others; not with people who have been where you want to go for years, but also not with those you've passed two years ago. No, such comparisons lead to nothing. Instead, it's all about one single thing: To grow as a person and give everything to be better than you were yesterday. To become the best version of yourself. To be awesome. Hidden inside yourself is so much potential you should never be satisfied with less. So many people carelessly waste away their talents because they tell themselves on a daily basis that it is impossible to be successful or to make a difference. What a misconception.

Imagine what would have happened if Michael Jordan hadn't spent so much time on the training grounds, but become a hobby basket ballplayer instead. If Eric Clapton didn't practice the guitar seven days a week, eight hours a day, but instead convinced himself that it was perfectly fine to only play at kids' school functions. If Salvador Dali didn't express his talents by way of exceptional paintings, but listened to surrounding objections and became a civil servant.

> Never compare yourself to other people. Become the best version of yourself instead.

It would fill my heart with joy if you would make a decision right here and right now to set out on the path to your own individual uniqueness. Use the fire inside of you to make an external difference and please don't ever be satisfied with mediocre just because it has become the social standard by now. Go full speed from where you are right now, or, to say it in the words of Martin Luther King, "If a man is called to be a street sweeper, he should sweep streets even as a Michelangelo painted, or Beethoven composed music or Shakespeare wrote poetry. He should sweep streets so well that all the hosts of heaven and earth will pause to say, 'Here lived a great street sweeper who did his job well.'"

By the way, Sir Ernest Shackleton's expedition failed. In the eternal cold of Antarctica, his ship, the *Endurance*, was squashed by heaps of pack ice, a few hundred miles before they reached the finish line. For almost an entire year, the crew lived on an ice floe and was hoping for it to drift north eventually. The men were sleeping in frozen sleeping bags and survived on penguin fat and their sled dogs, which they shot one at a time. When the ice floe threatened to break apart one day, the men saved themselves through a desperate operation, at first going onto an uninhabited island, before Shackleton and five of his companions set out to get help in a boat that was only twenty-two feet long. Indeed, after fifteen endless days they made it through the stormy Atlantic Ocean to a whale catching station in South Georgia. Another three months later, they picked up the rest of their team members from the island in a tugboat, almost two years after their daring departure into the ice. "I've made it," a telegram sent to Shackleton's wife said. "Not one life lost, on the way through hell."

Your Personal Declaration of Independence

Do you still feel up to the expedition to uniqueness after these words? Then I would like to introduce you to my ad:

"Brave men and women wanted for a breathtaking journey. No pay. Hard work. Entire months full of doubts and setbacks. Constant butting in from whiners, complainers and know-it-alls. Return to your old life impossible. Unbelievable freedom and satisfaction in return for the willingness to take full responsibility."

Are you on board? Great! But don't be deceived because, unfortunately, this path is not quite as easy as it may sound initially because we cling on to our heteronomous life way too much and we keep on sugarcoating the restrictions that seem almost obvious in retrospective. But, at some point, the signals become overwhelmingly clear, and we can't ignore them any longer because the fear of not changing overrides all convenience, excuses and habits by far. Then it's time to make a decision.

I remember the exact moment when I made my own personal declaration of independence. It was shortly after I started out as a store manager at Karstadt, right after I finished university. At the time, I was twenty-seven years old, completely inexperienced and quite shy. For the training on the job, I was assigned to an old warhorse called Werner Zeller. On our very first day together, he made a clear statement. "Grzeskowitz, congratulations that you've been to university, but here nobody cares. You better forget everything you learned there, because in the retail business there are different skills required." Today, I know that he was right, but back then I was completely intimidated.

Indeed, six months later, my situation hadn't improved at all and my whole emotional condition could easily be summed up by one word: Frustration. All my co-workers from the Trainee Program were getting promoted quickly and moving to exciting locations. I was the only one who was permanently on hold and one day I really became scared because I was promised a tiny little department store in a town called Duisburg Walsum that was planned to be shut down in the next year. But I kept on waiting for somebody to do something about it and wondered why things didn't improve. Then, one day, I had a lucky break. The manager of my dream department store was about to retire, and he needed a successor.

So I took all my courage, walked into the office of my boss and told him with all the determination I had, "Boss, nothing on Earth is as important to me as this position. We need to talk." So we talked. For about a minute. At first, he looked out of the window, and then he said, "Ilja, I know that you want to be in charge of that store, but, first of all, you aren't ready yet and, second, we definitely have better candidates than you. I'd rather see you in Duisburg Walsum." That was it. End of conversation. I still remember how disappointed I felt as I left the office. I was so frustrated that I said to my girlfriend, "I think I'm going to quit."

But, lucky for me, she answered, "Oh, my dear, of course you can do whatever you want. But I can't remember that I fell in love with a man who is a quitter."

That hit me. But it was the necessary impulse that I needed. And it started with taking responsibility. My boss was right. I wasn't ready yet and others were better than me because for far too long I had waited for others to do something and completely forgot to take action myself. In that moment, my whole frustration transformed into clarity and I swore to myself, "That will never happen again. Never in my whole life am I going to wait for others to be responsible for my career, my results and my future. From today on, I will roll up my sleeves and become so good that I can't be ignored!" And with this, my life was never going to be the same again.

> Formulate your personal declaration of independence. Start your inner rebellion and follow up with outside actions.

You're probably wondering whether I have solely been acting independently and responsibly since this declaration of independence; of course the answer is a resounding *No*. On the outside, everything went on as usual. Old habits die hard. But inside of me, an awareness that I had never known before started developing whenever I was doing something that went against my values, my beliefs and my core ideas about life. The more I was paying attention to this the less I was willing to just give up without a fight. I was thinking differently. I was deciding differently. And, increasingly, I started acting differently. But it was actually more than six years before I followed my inner rebellion with the deciding external actions, when I quit my job as a manager and started all over from scratch.

Sometimes it seems like irony of fate that, viewed from the outside, I was at the height of my career at that moment. At the same time, I had hit an absolute low point emotionally. But these intense emotions seemed to have been necessary to finally spring me into action. I like to talk about having two lives since then—an old life, in which I worked as an external-directed and mostly dissatisfied manager of a big company, and a new life, where I had to work my way up once more, and in which the initial times were pretty rough. But every single mile of this journey was worth it, because I feel an inner balance and satisfaction that I've only known since I've been thinking and acting on my own, according to my own visions; because I chose myself as the most important constant in a world of permanent changes. I had given myself the permission to be awesome.

Am I completely free? No, of course not. There are still situations in which my plans are based on the decisions of a customer, service provider or business partner. But the big difference is that I can chose this myself, at any time. Today I have the freedom to turn down a contract, award a needed service to another provider and consciously choose my business partners. Of course, this gift of choice is not without the obligation of responsibility. But believe me, I wouldn't want to trade this combination for the world.

I admit my consequence looks pretty radical from the outside and I definitely don't want to incite you to take a step like that in your life. There are plenty of opportunities to solve your inner conflicts in a different way. But I've always been a believer in "Walk your Talk". For years, I've done everything to give meaning to my job and to achieve the best possible results together with my team. But if you often feel like you cannot do anything else then the time has finally come to make a decision. Love it. Change it. Or leave it.

And this brings us to the next important point. There is a very reliable compass for making difficult decisions. I'm talking about values, the norms and rules that determine your daily life and that are a reliable guide in good and in bad times. So let us take a closer look at the power of values. Are you ready for the next stage of our expedition? Then it's time: Cast off! We're leaving port!

The Renaissance of Values

Why are you leading the life you lead? Why have you chosen your specific profession? What's your drive when things aren't going so well? The answer to these three questions is the same: It's your values. This subject has fascinated me for years, because nothing has such an impact on our decisions, behavior patterns and results as our inner value system. But what exactly do I mean by that? Wikipedia has the following definition: "Values can be defined as broad preferences concerning appropriate courses of action or outcomes. As such, values reflect a person's sense of right and wrong or what "ought" to be. Equal rights for all, Excellence deserves admiration, and People should be treated with respect and dignity are representative of values. Values tend to influence attitudes and behavior."

I like to get to the point a bit more and describe values as "desirable (or undignified) characteristics that serve as an assessment standard in our decision making." In order for you to get an even better understanding of this statement, I would like to introduce a short (and incomplete) list of values to you. Here, I differentiate between values that we strive for and that have a positive connotation to us, and those that we like to avoid and view as a negative.

Positive values from A - Z

Activity, Acceptance,	Challenge,	Conflict ability,
Affiliation, Altruism,	Cleanliness,	Concern, Courage,
Balance,	Creativity,	Democracy,
Belief,	Commitment,	Discipline,
Bravery,	Compassion,	Distance,
Care,	Competence,	Earnestness,
Career,	Composure,	Ease,
Change,	Comradery,	Education,
Charisma,	Confidence,	Eloquence,

Equality,
Fame,
Family,
Fantasy,
Freedom,
Friendship,
Frugality,
Fulfillment,
Fun,
Generosity,
Happiness,
Harmony,
Health,
Humanity,
Humility,
Home,
Humor,
Honesty,
Honor,
Hospitality,
Impartiality,
Independence,
Individuality,
Integrity,

Intelligence,
Justice,
Love,
Loyalty,
Luck,
Nonchalance,
Obedience,
Obligation,
Objectivity,
Openness,
Partnership,
Passion,
Peace,
Perseverance,
Personality,
Politeness,
Power,
Pragmatism,
Principle, Prudence,
Punctuality,
Reason,
Recognition,
Regulation,
Reliability

Respect,
Responsibility,
Safety,
Security,
Self-realization,
Sense of community,
Sense of duty,
Sexuality,
Sociability,
Solidarity
Spontaneity,
Straightforwardness,
Strength,
Success,
Superiority,
Taste,
Tenderness,
Tolerance,
Tradition,
Truth,
Warmth,
Wealth,
Wisdom,
Zest for life

Negative values from A - Z

Anger,
Arrogance,
Betrayal,
Boredom,
Brutality,
Conflict,
Cowardice,
Cruelty,
Deception,

Dependency Culture,
Despondency,
Disarray,
Disregard,
Dishonesty,
Dishonor,
Disloyalty,
Envy,
Failure,

Fault,
Fear,
Force,
Fraud,
Frustration,
Futility,
Gluttony,
Greed,
Hate,

Hostility,	Misfortune,	Suspicion,
Humility,	Monotony,	Stagnation,
Incompetence,	Naivety,	Standstill,
Indecisiveness,	Negativity,	Stinginess,
Infidelity,	Passivity,	Stress,
Insecurity,	Phoniness,	Stubbornness,
Intolerance,	Pigheadedness,	Stupidity,
Irresponsibility,	Pomposity,	Tardiness,
Jealousy,	Poverty,	Torture,
Lack of discipline,	Primitivism,	Unreliability,
Lack of freedom,	Rage,	Unrest,
Lack of humor,	Refusal,	Unsociability,
Lack of taste,	Rejection,	Violence,
Laziness,	Resentment,	Wastefulness,
Lethargy,	Resistance,	Weakness
Lies,	Ruthlessness,	
Loneliness,	Sickness,	

Have you let these two lists affect you a bit? Then I would like to ask you two questions:

1. What are your ten most important positive values?
2. Which ten values do you absolutely want to avoid in your life?

I really recommend taking some time for this reflection, and please be very aware of one thing. There is a huge difference between the values that we intellectually see as a positive and those that we actually live by and act on. You can put this to the test. Ask a hundred people what their most important values are, and at least ninety percent of the time you will receive "honesty" as the answer. But as soon as the next conflict situation arrives, there's much to be desired and people reach for

> Start your individual analysis of values. Create a list of positive and a list of negative ones.

white lies, keep information secret or are too afraid to voice an honest opinion out of fear of not being politically correct.

Only your actions are a direct mirror of your values. Nothing else. If punctuality was important to you, you would never be late. If honesty were an important value for you, you would rather deal with the negative consequences of not lying. If you viewed frugality as desirable, you would never randomly throw money around. Generally speaking, you can say that you can determine exactly what's important to you and what you'd rather avoid by looking at your values.

But back to the mirror. I've learned about the correlation between our values and the corresponding behavior the hard way, many years ago. For that you have to know that the value of family has always been high on all of my lists. Intellectually, it made perfect sense, because nothing was more important to me than my wife and my, back then very young, daughter. It was so important that I was constantly talking about it to my colleagues, co-workers and friends. And I still remember it today, the realization hitting me like a brick when a colleague I was friends with confronted me with the following statement: "Ilja, if family is so important to you, why are you still at the office at nine pm for the fourth time this week?" As a first instinct, I wanted to explain my reasons, wanted to argue that it was just an exception, but then I quickly realized that everything I could say would be a cheap excuse in the end—albeit a very logical and plausible excuse, but, as much as I wished it to be different, an excuse nontheless. And it took a lot of courage to admit the real reason why I was doing this to myself: Back then, my career simply was more important to me than my family.

I have to admit this realization ate away at me quite a bit because, in my mind, my family was the most important thing of all but my behavior showed something completely different. As the old wisecrack says, "I can't hear your words, your actions speak too loudly!" But I did not want to accept this situation and knew that I had to change something. Basically, I had two options. Either I had to change my hierarchy of values and accept the fact that, at that moment, my career was my highest priority, or I had to change my behavior to align with my values. And this is exactly what I chose to do, by no longer focusing on my time at the office, but on efficiency and results. The result was that I wasn't only more satisfied, but was working with more drive and fun.

I hope one thing became very clear through this example. Working on your own values sounds pretty simple and easy in theory. You write down a few desirable terms that sound good to you and you would like to have in your life. The problem is it doesn't matter at all what we write down on a piece of paper, the only thing that counts is always which values we act out of— and those aren't always identical with the ones we'd like to have. This is due to a simple, but often-overlooked, causation. We rate our own behavior, our ideas and values based on our intentions, but those of the people around us exclusively based on their results. If we used the same yardstick for ourselves, many of us would watch their entire view of the world collapse like a house of cards.

> We rate our own behavior, our ideas and values based on our intentions, but those of the people around us exclusively based on their results.

I would like to give you another example. Please imagine that your list includes the values peace and integrity right at the top. You are firmly convinced and, of course, would never act against your pacifist principles. But one day you find yourself in a dire situation. You've lost your job, have to pay back multiple loans and have four hungry kids at home that look at you full of hope with empty stomachs each night. Unfortunately, it's not that easy to find another job and your debts are slowly threatening to outgrow you.

Then, one day, you receive a phenomenal job offer—a management position with a company car, generous pension and a salary that exceeds your wildest expectations by far. You know you just have to say *Yes,* and all your problems would soon be solved. You would have a great, demanding job. Your debts would be gone at once and your family would have enough to eat again. But there's a catch. The job offer comes from an arms manufacturer that delivers weapons to various crisis regions in the world. How will you decide based on these prerequisites? Are your values important enough to you that you can renounce the financial security of your family without batting and eye, or were freedom and integrity more of a theoretical wishful thinking?

Even though this was just a hypothetical consideration, the decision really isn't easy, is it? And still we operate according to this principle daily. We have to make our decisions based on our individual value system, for small things as well as big things, at work, in our relationships and our everyday life. The more solidified your values are the easier it is to make a clear and irrefutable decision. As we will see later, every lasting change starts with exactly this. Therefore, I would like to get you excited about taking a critical, intense look at your personal and innermost values. Because any time your values and your behavior are in conflict with each other you feel a sense of dissatisfaction, feel like you are at a standstill or don't achieve the desired results. So here is my checklist for an optimal alignment of your individual value system.

Ten steps for the optimal alignment of your individual value system

1. Write down all the values that are important to you. Be creative. Brainstorm. And, as always, the best way to do this is with a pen and your change journal.
2. Pick the ten most important values from your list.
3. Arrange these values in hierarchical order, where your most important value is on top, your second most important value right below it, and so on.
4. Repeat the whole thing with your negative values that you want to avoid at all costs.
5. Check if any values on the lists are in conflict with each other (for example: freedom and security or recognition and rejection). Should you come across a conflict of values, replace the lesser important value with a motivating alternative.
6. Check if your daily behavior is in harmony with your most important values. Should you come across a conflict, you have two options. First: You replace a value with a new one that fits your behavior. Second: You consciously adjust your behavior based on the value.
7. Adapt your list until you have twenty values in total that reflect your biggest dreams, views and attributes and fit with your future (dream) life.
8. Integrate your (new) values into your daily life and consciously pay attention to acting according to your most important values when making decisions.
9. Do this until your consciously chosen value system has become an automated and habitual basis for your decisions and your behavior.
10. In the beginning, repeat the process every four months, later, once a year.

The more you deal with your very own individual values the more you will realize how important this piece of the puzzle is in expressing your extraordinary personality. The more you are able to fall back on strong and deeply rooted values the more you will be perceived as a Changemaker, because you are living the *Think it. Do it. Change it.* philosophy with every fiber of your being.

Even though every person in the world has their very own individual value system, there are a few universal values that interconnect all Changemakers.

The most important ones are:

> There are some universal values every Changemaker should incorporate in his life.

Changemaker value #1: Personal responsibility

This phrase is probably used the most in my books and for a good reason. Nothing is as important as taking responsibility for your own ideas, decisions and actions. Without exception. Without compromise. Without excuses.

Changemaker value #2: Courage

Those who dare to leave the beaten paths and implement change without a title, money or permission inevitably need a lot of courage. Why? It's simple; new ideas are often laughed at in the beginning and often even fought.

Changemaker value #3: Responsibility for others

True Changemakers are always individual personalities, but also take responsibility for their co-workers, colleagues, friends and family members without any debate. Why? Because they know that success is only possible in a team!

Changemaker value #4: The ability to make decisions

Always make your decisions on time, clearly and straightforward. Nothing gives your environment (and yourself) a clearer orientation than the certainty that you are able to make a decision. Later, we will take a closer look at how this works exactly.

Changemaker value #5: Clarity

Don't dilly-dally, but stand by your word, your decisions and your opinions. The clearer you communicate the more reliable you are as a boss, co-worker, friend or partner.

Changemaker value #6: Discipline

Don't think hard work is beneath you, and do everything to reach the goals you have set for yourself. This requires a huge amount of discipline. Do you remember the quote by Brancusi? "Create like a God. Command like a king. Work like a slave."

But it's not just positive values that connect the Changemakers of this world with each other, there are also some that you should definitely avoid. In my opinion, these negative values are the biggest hurdles to success that exist.

Success hurdle #1: Envy

This value is a sign of an inner deficiency that you should definitely leave behind. Whenever you experience an inkling of this feeling (and you will, because, after all, you aren't a robot) then turn it right around. Be happy for the person you envy from the bottom of your heart. If you would like to have what they achieved or reached, ask yourself, *What do I have to do in order to achieve the same thing?* This is the way of thinking that will lead you to success.

Success hurdle #2: Negativity

I'm definitely not a fan of constantly walking around with rose-colored glasses on, but there's one thing I know for sure: Those who constantly see everything in a negative light, concentrate on complaining, whining and badmouthing, will obstruct their own success. Try implementing the following formula instead: Recognize problems, analyze your starting situation and then put all your efforts into possible solutions.

Success hurdle #3: Dependency culture

How does my respected colleague Randy Gage put it? "The only free cheese is in the mousetrap!" Or to rephrase: Nothing in life is "free". Please never rely on thinking that you are entitled to something that others have to earn. At the end of the day, this dependency culture leads to passiveness, lethargy and the transfer of responsibilities.

Success hurdle #4: Playing the victim

Whenever things go wrong, it's the easiest thing in the world to feel like you're a victim of outside circumstances and start looking for the fault in others. Don't fall into this trap, but take responsibility for your results, especially when failures happen.

Was I able to interest you a bit in the subject of values? I'm always surprised that so few people intensively deal with their inner motivation. And you should have realized by now how much our daily actions are controlled by our values, especially in a world that seems to drift into arbitrariness more and more; strong and explicit values are a rare exception that clearly set apart a company, organization or person from their environment. That's why I will never tire of calling out for a renaissance of values any time I possibly can. It would be a great honor if you would follow my call. Your uniqueness will thank you.

Ten Minutes in the Olympic Stadium

A few days ago, on a flight, I watched one of my favorite movies: *Walk the Line*, it's a beautiful documentary of the life story of Johnny Cash, played by Joaquin Phoenix. Even though the entire movie is brilliant, one single scene sticks out. It's at the very beginning of Johnny Cash's career, when he has the opportunity to play in front of the producer Sam Phillips; the still largely unknown musician and his little band played it safe and chose a pretty popular gospel song, which they performed more or less free of emotions. They were quickly interrupted and a dispute ensued.

Johnny complained, "Well, you never let us bring it home."

Sam Phillips replied, "Bring it home. Okay, let's bring it home. If you was hit by a truck and you were lying out in a gutter and you had time to sing one song—one song that people would remember before you're dirt, one song that would let God know what you felt about your time here on Earth, one song that would sum you up—are you telling me that's the one song you'd sing? That same Jimmy Davis tune that we hear on the radio all day about your peace within and how it's all real and how you're gonna shout it. Or would you sing something different, something real, something you felt? Cause I'm telling you right now, that's the kind of song people want to hear. That's the kind of song that truly saves people. It ain't got nothing to do with believing in God, Mr. Cash, it has everything to do with believing in yourself!"

Johnny Cash understood the message. He rid himself of all the external constraints and expectations and truly listened to himself. And what he heard was anything but an ideal world, rose-colored cloud or arbitrariness. Deep inside of himself he felt a lot of pain, disappointment and bitterness, a potent cocktail of emotions that he turned into a song that he never dared to sing for many years. But the right time had come and he sang a song called *Folsom Prison Blues* that would later make him rich and famous. It was only when he allowed himself to express his inner uniqueness that his success translated on the outside.

May I share with you one of my core beliefs? Every single person has something deep inside of himself or herself that makes him or her extraordinary. Every single person has unique talents and abilities. Every single person has the opportunity to use his or her own personal story to make a difference. What is it that makes you extraordinary? What do you hear if you listen deep inside of yourself? "Honestly, Ilja," people say to me a lot, "I can't hear anything, and I'm neither special nor extraordinary." Does this sound familiar to you? I can relate, because there was a time in my life when I thought the exact same way. I had a job that frustrated me, was driven by external circumstances, and was constantly finding plausible excuses why I definitely wasn't able to change anything.

This change happened after my personal declaration of independence. I had decided to finally take responsibility for my life. But the corresponding results were a long time coming, because I was still searching for my mission, my uniqueness, my personal purpose in life. And then I was saved by television. Yes, I'm serious. I had just started my own business when I saw a show with the famous German comedian Mario Barth one evening in my hotel room. It was a performance in front of 70.000 people in the Olympic stadium in Berlin, which earned him the Guinness World Record in the category *Comedy show with the largest live audience.* Initially, I was mainly fascinated by his performance. Mario Barth had managed to make it from a small theatre stage (where he performed regularly in front of thirty people) to the biggest sports arena in Germany. I thought this was more than impressive and was asking myself what kind of mindset might be part of such a path.

I can't remember exactly what impulse was responsible for it, but suddenly another question popped into my head. *If you had the opportunity to speak in front of 70.000 people in the Olympic stadium for ten minutes, what exactly would you say?* It was another one of those questions that would prove to be a turning point in my life, because, in order to answer it, I had to start searching for my inner core, brush all insignificant details aside and find the very message that I was convinced other people should hear. I pondered for weeks and months, sorted through and thought about possible answers. And, step-by-step, my thoughts solidified until that one day came and I was clear about what I would say if I ever got the chance to speak in front of 70.000 people. Do you want to know what it is? Here's my message, summarized in a single sentence:

"Every single person has huge potential hidden inside of them that's just waiting to be discovered. The key to this kingdom is individual uniqueness; the path to get there is change."

Since that day, it has been my big mission in life to support people to become the best version of themselves and not to see change as something that's threatening, but as a huge opportunity to actively shape their future, grow as a person and achieve lasting results. From one moment to the next, all pieces of the puzzle fell into place. I had discovered my individual uniqueness and I gave myself permission to express it, to be awesome every single day.

> The key to your full potential is your uniqueness. The path to get there is change.

If you met me at one of my speeches or seminars today, many years later, you would feel how passionate I still am about my message and my mission. My job gives me the opportunity to express this inner passion on a daily basis, every moment and with every fiber of my being with what I say, write and how I conduct myself. All this leads to a combined package that others like to describe as authentic or charismatic. Personally, I prefer the word extraordinary.

The best thing about it is I have been lucky enough to see and be a part of this same transformation of many other people. Maybe you've heard this corny saying before, that successful people aren't born, they are made. For me, that's the biggest BS I've ever heard. People are never made from the outside, they develop from the inside out. You go down your individual path to uniqueness and then you live it with every fiber of your being. At work. In your daily life. Always. This formula for success is pretty simple. Allow yourself to recognize your own unique personality, bring it out and make it your biggest motivator. And if you happen to find ways for other people to profit from your uniqueness then you have opened the gates to success, fulfillment and satisfaction. After all, what could be better than making your uniqueness the deciding crux of the matter in your life and making a profit on top of it all?

So, in closing this chapter, let us talk about the deciding question: What is your uniqueness, what sets you apart from others? If you can't think of an answer right away that's completely normal. Always remember that we are talking about a process that can take many years. A good starting point is to take a look at your past. What have you experienced, what have you done, what have you achieved? Please remind yourself of this fact as often as you can: The miles you have walked in life, nobody can take them away from you. They are the basis for everything that is yet to be. And they are worth being talked about, and expressed. If you don't do it, nobody will. And the world would be missing something very important.

If you'd like to dig a little deeper to get to your inner core, the following questions are a good guideline:

Questions that help you to find your inner core

- What's your *Why* in life?
- What gives your body an automatic burst of energy?
- What makes you stay up and work all hours of the night?

- What do you want to be remembered for?
- What would you like to be written on your headstone one day?
- What makes your eyes light up?
- What was the lowest point in your life?

These thoughts trigger your creativity and prepare your for the most important consideration:

"If you had the chance to speak in front of 70.00 people or more at the biggest stadium in your home town for ten minutes, what exactly would you say?"

Reject being like everyone else and go your own way. Become the best version of yourself. There is a unique core that is just waiting to be expressed with every fiber of your being in what you think, what you say, what you decide and what you do, at your job, in your private life and every second of your life. The result is what people today like to call authenticity. Simply extraordinary.

Another important piece of information: Please forget striving for perfection. Nobody likes perfect people. And if you appear too smooth and unflawed, you will automatically encounter rejection. Every one of us has their weaknesses, their quirks and weird characteristics. But it is exactly these rough edges that make us so extraordinary. Have the courage to be as authentic as possible, take down your various masks and be as human as possible. Nobody has said it better than the Korean artist Nam June Paik, who spoke a warning to all those people who were too focused on the ideal of perfection in 1993. "When too perfect, God angry!"

Be courageous enough to show your imperfections. Dare to express your uniqueness in your job, your ideas and every single one of your actions. Just as Johnny Cash found his one, life changing song with a little help from producer Sam Phillips, I would hope that this book serves as the deciding push for you, to seek out your inner core.

> Find your unique core. You don't have to be perfect. Quite the contrary: "When too perfect, God angry" (Nam June Paik).

I don't know how exactly your uniqueness will look. All I know is that it will be different, it will be real and it will be something that you feel deep inside of you. When all these factors come together, you create the basis for extraordinary results. Johnny Cash has touched millions of hearts with his uniqueness. His courage to be authentic made him successful and famous. Which way will you go?

Chapter Summary

> *Think it. Do it. Change it.* The big ideas of this chapter
>
> ✓ If you allow yourself to live your own uniqueness you have taken the deciding step that sets you apart from the masses
> ✓ You as a person can either be invisible or extraordinary
> ✓ Consciously taking risks has long become the new safe
> ✓ You yourself are the only factor that you will always be able to rely on during times of change
> ✓ Take responsibility and draft your personal declaration of independence
> ✓ Your actions are a mirror of your values
> ✓ The clearer your values are, the easier it is to make decisions
> ✓ Integrate the Changemaker values into your life and bid goodbye to the biggest hurdles of success
> ✓ If you had the opportunity to speak in front of 70.000 people at the Olympic stadium for ten minutes, what exactly would you say?
> ✓ Dare to show your imperfections. When too perfect, God angry.

The Four Pillars of Change -
Why Only the Relentless Are Rewarded with Results

"Pain throws your heart to the ground. Love turns the whole thing around. No it won't all go the way it should. But I know the heart of life is good."

- John Mayer, Heart of Life

Every time has its trends. In the 1980s it was the Walkman, roller-skates and the epic hymns of Bon Jovi. In the 1990s there was the Tamagotschi, soccer players wore a haircut named Mullet and techno was played on the dance floors around the world. And today there is a Zeitgeist, which I have observed in an almost inflationary manner in the past few weeks. No matter what book I open, which Facebook post I read or which expert opinion I listen to, I keep hearing the same message. Summarized in my own words, it goes something like this: "In order to be successful and lead a happy life, it is necessary to stop thinking and (finally) listen to your heart." Most of the time the famous quote from the book *Little Prince* by de Saint-Exupéry is added, in order to give more emphasis to the message. "It is only with the heart that one can see rightly. What is essential is invisible to the eye." And the reaction to this thesis is usually one and the same. Like Pavlov's dogs, the people cheer with the rest of the masses and are happy that someone is finally saying what they've suspected for so long: All that counts is your heart, the rest really does not matter.

The devil is in the details. Because at first glance this statement sounds enticingly logic. "Listen to your heart and everything will be fine." And there's a lot of truth to it. But, unfortunately, there's a lot of untruth as well. Of course, we find our motivation in our hearts; what is truly important to us makes us get up every morning. However, this draws some wrong conclusions, namely that, once you listen to your heart, you can completely disregard your mind.

You can observe the results of this deception daily, most likely in your own environment as well. Some throw away their jobs as bankers, tax specialists or electricians from one day to the next because their heart tells them that they should finally follow their calling. What this looks like exactly they don't really know yet, but at least their boring job isn't restricting them any longer, and they can express their personality (most of the time in some activity in the helping industry, because then you don't have to look after yourself). Suddenly, they are a life coach, owner of a nail salon or organizer of motivational seminars for pet owners—of course, without any kind of commercial knowledge, a concrete business plan or realistic consideration of the market opportunities.

But just as fast as the fire of desire was lit, a very hard realization happens. It might be quite nice to do something you wholeheartedly enjoy, but if it doesn't pay your bills and it's putting you in a financial bind, the romance that was so strong before fades quickly. And this relates to one thing. Without your mind, the best decision of the heart is worth nothing. If other people find no use in your personal passion, you won't earn any money. And if you don't generate any income then it might be a nice hobby, but not a profession.

This is why I would like to encourage you at this point never to forget to use your mind when it comes to the decisions in your life. Yes, I'm even going to go a bit further and would like to express a declaration of love to the human mind. It is the most precious gift that we have. Our mind lets us balance chances and risks. It lets us critically question things and draw our own conclusions. It lets us develop ideas and create inventions. It lets us decide and act. And the more we use our mind, the better our decisions and results will be.

So should we start listening only to our minds from now on? No, quite the opposite. Because as the Yin is nothing without the Yang, the mind and heart need one another. Only when they work together are people able to develop their full potential and become a unique person. Only the combination of heart and mind makes it possible for you to become the best version of yourself, step by step. No matter what it is you want to achieve, the heart is always the motor. It reliably tells you when it is time for a change. It shows you when something is wrong. It is the deciding driving force to get moving. And your mind ensures that you walk down your chosen path the best possible way you can; that you don't walk through life with your rose-colored glasses, but also don't meet trouble halfway; that you don't ignore potential problems, but still focus on the chances that present themselves.

Let us get specific now. How do you imagine your future? Which dreams do you have; what would you like to achieve; where would you like to be in two years? What, you haven't really thought about that? Until now you've taken everything as it came? Then it is definitely time for a change because one thing is for certain. The next years are definitely going to arrive. The only question is will you leave the course of time and especially its results up to chance, or will you be self-determined and actively create your success, your luck and your satisfaction? The second alternative is, without a doubt, the one that will promise much better results, because, as Bob Dylan sang in 1964, "The times, they are a-changing." So, whenever you try out this can-do attitude in practice in the near future, I want you to remember the following mantra: "Listen to your heart. But don't forget about your mind!"

> On your individual way to greatness, the combination of heart and mind is like Yin and Yang.

Nothing is as powerful as the combination of a rational analysis and emotionally-driven actions. Logic lets you understand and emotions let you take action. In conclusion, it's always about integrating the desired changes into your daily life over the long term. And right at this point is where most of my audience members, seminar participants and coaching customers fail. Maybe you are familiar with this as well. With high motivation, you start in to a change. But after a short period of time, the pressure of your daily life gets too heavy and you fall right back into your old habits.

Before you know it, you are right back in your old rut and have made yourself comfortable in your personal comfort zone because you aren't quite sure where you should start, what your first steps should look like, or how you can keep at it over time. Does this sound familiar? Then I would like to introduce you to the four most important pillars of lasting change. They are the foundation, the basis and the topsoil, where your future success will grow. Take as much time as you need for each step because, at the end of the day, an expert is always a person who has mastered the fundamentals and can reiterate the basics in his sleep.

The four pillars of lasting change

1st pillar: A conscious "Oh yeah" to change
2nd pillar: An irrevocable decision
3rd pillar: A clear goal
4th pillar: A strong habit

These four pillars build the foundation for a successful transformation from vague ideas to specific results. They make sure that you not only start highly motivated, but also reach the finish line.

Say, "Oh Yeah!" To Change

How about the current priorities in your life? What's important to you, and which projects are you most passionate about? Is it your career, your health, your family or something completely different? If you aren't quite sure, just take a look at your current life situation. It is completely determined by your focus. Your time, energy and money go to what is important to you. You get more of what you focus on. That's true for every single area of your life.

I learned that lesson over twelve years ago from a wonderful woman. She was an actress and the seminar leader of a workshop for department store managers, which I had to attend. If you had been there, you would have described her external appearance as *a lot like Cameron Diaz*. But after she said her first words, you would have recognized her attitude is more like Margaret Thatcher. I think my boss knew that, because for day two of the program, he had a very special idea: Improv theatre for leaders. That meant being creative. Being spontaneous. Permanently testing your limits. That, in turn, meant for me: Heart palpitations. Breaking out in a cold sweat. Gasping for air. Why, you ask? Simple, if you had known me back then, you could have described me with many words, but none of them would have been spontaneous, creative or flexible.

And it couldn't have started worse. Do you know that feeling when you get to the edge of your comfort zone? I found myself exactly there, when the first assignment started. Margaret Diaz was standing in front of the group, and, with a smile on her face, she said, "Okay guys, I'm going to give you some very uncommon exercises. And no matter what you think of each exercise, I want you to react by powerfully shouting these two words: *Oh Yeah!* and then do the exercise. All right?"

Picture the situation. A beautiful woman is standing in front of you and says, "Now everyone jumps on one leg." And fifty more or less experienced leaders shout in unison, *"Oh Yeah!"* and then all jump on one leg. Now be honest, would you have participated? I did not do it because I found it far too embarrassing. Next, she announced, "Now everyone is going to spin around in a circle." My colleagues shouted again, *"Oh Yeah!"* and started spinning, while I was trying with all my might not to stand out. But I had a gut feeling that the best was yet to come. And I was right, because she said, "And now everyone hugs the person standing next to him." *"Oh Yeah!"* The battle cry filled the room once again, and, to my left, a 247 pound colleague with a full beard named Manfred was extending both his arms and was about to hug me.

And it must have been the look on my face, because suddenly the pretty actress was standing in front of me. And she said something that made me think, *Ilja, what are you afraid of? Maybe it will be really good. But you'll never know unless you give it a try.* And as suddenly as she appeared, she disappeared again. And I was standing there. I hesitated. I had doubts. What should I do? Should I quit and leave the room or should I be bold and give it a try? And it felt like eternity to me, until I made my decision. Actually, she was right. The least I could do was give it a try to see what would happen. And so even if I still had doubts, I said, "Oh yeah!" and hugged Manfred, who very tenderly cuddled himself against me.

> Whatever challenges you are facing, say *Oh Yeah!* as often as possible.

And you know what? It wasn't bad at all. Quite the contrary. Because suddenly we got to know each other and later we even became very good friends. Since that day, I've looked at these two words as a fantastic metaphor on how to deal with change because every single day is full of *Oh Yeah!*

moments, when we deliberately need to choose our focus. Do we complain or do we roll up our sleeves? Do we whine or do we take action? Do we focus on problems or on solutions? After all, change is never what happens around us, but always how we deal with it in our minds.

I would like to encourage you to try this philosophy by yourself. Think about an important goal, an upcoming task or something that you are bit afraid of. Then say, *Oh Yeah!* with utter conviction and let yourself be taken by surprise. (Yes, you should really do this, nobody is watching.) Many of my customers are surprised how powerful the use of *Oh Yeah!* can be. Some of them laugh a bit initially, because they feel silly, but, in the end, I watch them secretly mumble these words over and over.

The more you make *Oh Yeah!* part of your daily life the more you will realize how much your focus shifts, how many possibilities you observe and how much you notice that you are enjoying your life more. But this is just an initial step. After all, what good is it if you notice all the possibilities hidden in a single change but don't make something out of them? And this is exactly where pillar number two comes into play.

Choose to Make a Decision

How many people do you know who are world champions in announcing, planning and taking to the task of changes, but then regularly fail when it comes to implementing them? How many times have you had a great idea but weren't able to put it into practice? It might surprise you, but most people who struggle with these kinds of issues don't have a problem with taking action, but rather a problem with making a decision. This is the result of wishy-washy values, and the lack of clear priorities that goes along with them. The consequences are fatal. After a while, you get used to the fact that other people will make the decisions for you. Your boss, your colleagues, your spouse, your neighbor, the store clerk and even the nice lady at the hotel check-in desk. You believe that nearly anyone is able to make a decision for you. You are the only person who fears that like the devil fears holy water. You will be able to recognize these undecided people by the way they talk, because they tend to overuse their two favorite words, *actually* and *maybe*. If you maybe think about actually wanting to change, you don't really have to make a decision about it. And that is exactly what most people want.

But why is this? Why does nobody want to commit themselves anymore? Why are so many people struggling to make a decision? For one, your own values definitely play a central role in this. If I don't know what the priorities in my life are then I can't act accordingly. If I'm uncertain on the inside, it is impossible to make clear decisions on the outside. But in most cases it's not even that someone is not able to commit themselves. It's usually the will to do it. You see there is one central feature in every decision. Whenever you make a decision about something, at the same time you are making a decision against something, with all the consequences, sacrifices and conflicts but also with the corresponding results. During every single decision we evaluate where our priorities lie. It always comes down to the question of what's more important to you. It's either ... or. Would you like a few examples?

- You can either have the freedom of having your own business or the (alleged) security of a permanent position
- You can either make that important call to a customer or check your status updates on Facebook for the tenth time today
- You can either work out early in the morning to get your dream body or spend another hour in your warm, cozy bed
- You can either plan the next steps in your career or spend the evening at the movies with your friends
- You can either work some overtime for an important project or enjoy the relaxing effects of ten hours of sleep
- You could either do anything to get that position as a manager that you so desire or you can insist on a punctual end of day
- You can either enjoy a romantic vacation with your spouse or travel to a spring break party with your friends
- You can either spend time with your kids or spend every night in the office until ten pm
- You can work on making your dreams reality or you can hit the clubs and enjoy the nightlife in your city

It always comes down to one question: "What is more important to you?" If you know what it is, it won't be as hard to commit. The more you fall back on powerful values and the more motivation 4.0 you have integrated into your life the sooner you will be willing to do anything to reach your goals. And because this requires work, discipline and commitment, most people are not willing to deal with these consequences.

But why is that? Today we live in a society that is marked by mediocrity. It is with great concern that I watch the trend of the masses to have their cake and eat it, too. Therefore, you do a little bit of everything but nothing properly. You maneuver your way through your own life without any major low points, but also without any highlights. It's the classic definition of mediocre. If you finally pull yourself together and make a decision, it usually isn't one because most people define the term rather loosely. If you look closer at them, most decisions turn out to be little more than a pipe dream that you hopefully cast toward the sky.

Please do not be fooled by this because a true decision is something completely different. It means to commit, with neck and crop, to the consequences of these actions and not be led astray by setbacks. Making a real decision means to be sure, to vote for something—and against the alternative, at the same time. It means to make a conscious choice. And many people shy away from this clear and consequent choice and would rather be led by external circumstances, or, worse, by the decisions of other people.

I'm definitely not only talking about the directive decisions in life. No, it starts with small things in your everyday life, while shopping, eating, riding the subway or at the dinner table. But those who let themselves be led by arbitrariness during these common daily things will fail at the big decisions in life all the more because, in the end, every single decision starts with a clear and irrevocable decision. The decision to make a change, to start on your way and enjoy the ride on this roller coaster called life with all its highs and lows.

> Every decision you make for something is a decision against something at the same time.

So let's cut to the chase, dear readers, how do your feel about how good or bad your decision making power is? If you aren't quite sure, you can put this to the test. Think about your last visit to a restaurant for a moment. How do you typically act? It is easy to pick a dish of your choice, or do you beat around the bush, study the menu from front to back, only to end up ordering the same thing as your neighbor, or the meal that the waiter suggests? How many times have you answered choice questions, like, "Would you like coffee or tea?" "Do you want to go to the movies or see a play?" or "Italian or Thai food?" with a terse, "I don't care," "You can choose," or "I like them both"?

Should you catch yourself during one of these avoidance behaviors, you need to be careful because if you are already having trouble making small decisions, this won't be any different when it comes to the important things in life. And every successful change eventually starts with an irrevocable decision. You cannot get around this. But I also have good news; it's not that hard to train your decision making skills. The basics are powerful values, which we have already talked about in depth. They always form the foundation that everything else aligns with. Additionally, I would like to provide you with a powerful guideline that can be a good orientation when it comes to future decisions.

Seven steps to better deal with changes

Step #1: Decide to make a decision

Sounds trivial, but it is the most important step of them all. From now on, we won't be messing around any longer, but start to make a decision—always, during the small decisions in everyday life as well as the important challenges. The sooner you make your new decisiveness a habit the better.

Step #2: Analyze your initial situation and weigh your options

Make an open and honest analysis of your current situation. Don't sweet-talk anything, but also don't make it seem worse than it is. The better you know where you stand the easier it will be to find possible options.

Step #3: Accept the fact that you will never know for sure which decision is right or wrong

This realization can save you a lot of brooding. Accept the fact that you will never know ahead of time which decision is the right one. Unfortunately, we only know that afterwards. But maybe this is a good thing, because, after all, experiences help us grow.

Step #4: Combine your knowledge with your intuition and make a decision

Here the unbeatable duo *Heart & Mind* comes into play again. Use your rational thinking as well as your gut feeling. Over the last few years, I have made nearly all the important decisions of my life based on my intuition. I have been doing very well with this strategy because every gut feeling works especially well when it is based on a sound and rational analysis.

Step #5: Take full responsibility for the consequences of your decision

This is a very important step, especially when other people are affected by the decision. Nothing builds trust quite like reliability and clarity. So, no matter what results may come of your decision, take responsibility—for the good things, but also for those that didn't go quite as well.

Step #6: Stand by your decision, even if you encounter resistance

When you take responsibility, you earn a bunch of respect and sometimes even admiration. On the other hand, nothing is more despicable than the constant changing of your opinions. Still, many people would prefer to take the easy way out and act like a flag in the wind, twist and turn whenever they can and eventually end up with a spine made out of rubber. Make one thing very clear to yourself: You won't be able to please everyone, and, most of the time, the right decisions are the least popular ones.

Step #7: Be courageous enough to revise your decision sometimes

Despite it all, it's important to be flexible when it comes to results. Sometimes you make the wrong decision. That's when it's important to react in time and make a new decision. You not only show that you can be open and honest with yourself, but also that you are a person of integrity.

I hope that you give these seven steps a chance and make them part of your daily life as a habit. Practice making decisions as often as you can.

Avoid the popular "wishy-washy" behavior and commit to small things as well as big things. Every single change starts with an irrevocable decision. A right one at that. Including all the consequences. A decision that involves commitment, motivation and discipline. A decision for which you are willing to do anything in your power to put it into practice.

Are you S.E.C.S.I. enough?

"Could I have a word with you real quick?" This is what a pleasant gentleman asked me after a book signing I held in southern Germany at the beginning of last year. "Of course," I answered, "what can I do for you?" And what happened next is something I encounter almost daily. Within three minutes, he had told me, in short, everything that was going wrong in his life. He was especially frustrated with the relationship he had with his wife, who he was currently going through a divorce with, and he kept working himself up due to these bad feelings.

At some point, he was just going in a circle, so I interrupted him. "I understand the current relationship with your wife is making you very unhappy. What exactly is it that I can help you with?" And right away he started telling the whole story all over again, this time with a lot more detail. I interrupted him once more and asked him again, "Okay, so what exactly are you expecting from our conversation?"

"Well", he said, "there's got to be some sort of technique that keeps me from being so frustrated all the time."

"It does exist," I answered truthfully, "what is it that you are you trying to achieve with this technique?" And the whole spiel started all over again. With each circle that the pleasant gentleman turned in, he was more focused on his problem and was desperately hoping to get advice from me.

In that moment, I realized that his real problem was lying completely elsewhere. He didn't know what he wanted at all. He didn't even ask himself what he wanted to replace his frustration with, and how he was imagining the improved relationship with his wife in the future. Maybe this is something that you are familiar with. You know exactly what you don't

> To achieve lasting changes, you need to have a clear and compelling goal.

want anymore, but you cannot say for certain what you want to achieve instead of this.

But how are you going to successfully change if you don't know what the results of your intentions should look like? Therefore, in this next step we want to talk about the important subject of goals. But don't worry, I won't torture you with the familiar (and unfortunately not effective) goal formulas, nor will we drift into theory. My intention is simple; I want you to integrate the third pillar of successful change into your life as forcefully as possible, so you can lead the life you've always dreamed of. Are you ready to begin?

All I need from you now is a brutally honest answer to the following question. "How happy are you currently in the following areas, on a scale from one to ten (one stands for *not at all* and ten for *could not get any better*)?

- Job
- Family
- Relationship
- Personal development
- Health
- Finances

I'm not interested in politically correct, socially acceptable or bloomy phrases. Instead, I want to know what you really feel and how you are doing. And if you give me a superficial response anyway then I can live with that too, because this isn't about me, but exclusively about you. You can fool others but you cannot lie to the person you see in the mirror every morning forever.

The more honest you are with yourself, the easier it is to make a correction in your course. Would you like to answer again? Good. If you are dissatisfied with any area of your life, have reached a certain level of frustration or would like to achieve more then it is time to make a change. But what goals do you have? What do you dream of? What is the vision that drives you?

As soon as that, we have reached the crucial point. Most people know very well what they don't want to deal with anymore, but they don't have a clue what should replace these things. After you've made the irrevocable choice to change, it is important to make the next step and clearly define what your specific results should look like. To help you with that, I would like to introduce to you a successful process that I use with my coaching clients on a regular basis in order to find out what they truly want. It always starts with this question: "What do you want to be, do or have in the future?" The answers that follow can be divided into six different categories:

The six categories of intention

1. Dream (I would like to be rich; I would like to start my own business; I would like to be successful)
2. Vision (I will be the best car salesman in Miami; Our brand is successful and known all over America; My company has a revenue of one million dollars and is the market leader in xyz)
3. Direction (I would like to do something in the media field; We will intensify our marketing efforts; I will spend more time with my family)
4. Goal (We will employ ten new apprentices by March 31st; I will sell 50.000 books in 2016; I will loose eight pounds by the end of the year)
5. Plan (I will call five clients per day; I will work out four times a week according to the workout plan xyz; I will spend six hours a day writing my new book)
6. Doing! (Achieving, implementing, taking action)

And here is the thing. The higher we are on the list the bigger our level of abstraction and emotional drive. The further down we are the more specific it gets, while our emotions start to decrease. Normally, we run through these six steps sequentially. A dream becomes a vision, which eventually leads to a vague direction. The more you move along the path the clearer your individual goals become, which then develop into a specific plan that you implement in the end. You just do it.

Sometimes, a vision or a vague direction is so riddled with emotions that you start taking action without any detours, and think about your goal and plans afterwards. But it doesn't matter how exactly your path looks, because, in the end, it all comes down to transforming your intentions into specific action steps and turning your dreams into concrete results.

Thus, let us start with exactly this. If you know where you want to go and start the path in time, this is the important next step for lasting changes. But many people fail right at this point because they don't have the right answer to the following question: "Where do I really want to go?" Have you asked yourself this question before, maybe pretty recently? Then I would like to introduce you to a wonderful exercise that will help you bring structure and clarity to your wishes, visions, directions, goals or plans.

> It's not enough to know what you don't want anymore. You also have to know what you want to replace it with.

And this is how it works. Get out your change journal and take some time for an extensive brainstorming of your future. Ask yourself the following question: "What do I want to be, do or have in the future?" And then get started. Write down everything that you can think of. Without any kind of rating. Let your pen run over the paper and let your inner fire burn. What did you always want to do? What did you want to achieve? What kind of goals do you have? Write for at least fifteen minutes and really write down everything, no matter how small and insignificant it may seem.

After you've completed this exercise, I recommend having a cup of coffee or taking a walk. Then read over the results of your brainstorming once again, and write the number one or two next to every goal.

- One stands for: This goal is very important to me. I will definitely go for it and take action to achieve it.
- And two means: I'm letting go of this goal.

Maybe you're asking yourself now, *What, I'm supposed to let go of my goal, why did I even write it down?* But you will see how important this step can be for you. There are quite some goals that we carry around for years, like a heavy backpack, and keep putting off making them reality. Isn't that true? Always remember there is a reason why you haven't realized this goal yet. There is a time for everything. And now you need your strength and energy for your new and current plans.

Let's keep going with the process. Next, write down your number one and number two goals on separate pieces of paper, so you now have a list of current goals and a list of no-longer-current goals. The time has come to say goodbye to the *old* ones. Think up a nice ritual and burn the list, for example in the fire pit in your garden or a fireproof flowerpot. Trust me, this is neither embarrassing nor esoteric, but truly freeing and power bestowing. And we now use this new energy to work on the realization of your current plans.

Get out your number one list and write either an "L", an "M" or an "S" next to each goal. The letters are divided into the following categories:

L = Long-term goal with a timescale of two to five years
M = Medium-term goal with a timescale of twelve months
S = Short-term goal with a timescale of four weeks

You will use your long-term goals as the compelling vision for your future. Fine-tune each wording until a wave of strong emotions overcomes you at the mere thought of it. The more emotional your association with your goal becomes the bigger the likelihood that you are willing to do anything to achieve it. For the greatest possible effect, I recommend developing a strong vision for very single area of your life. Many of my clients have achieved huge successes by hanging up their vision in their office, by way of a poster (vision board), or by putting a piece of paper with their vision written on it in their wallet. The more you think about it (consciously or subconsciously) the sooner your ideas, decisions and dreams will result in specific and massive action.

But because we are talking about a timeline of two to five years, it is important that you set yourself a few milestones on the way. This is where the medium and short-term goals come into play. Go through all your plans in this category and, for each one, imagine how it will feel when you have achieved this milestone. One important thing applies here as well, the more emotional the better.

Now, take out another empty piece of paper and write down your three most important goals. Should you still have any trouble during this step, go back and read the paragraph about making decisions again.

This brings us the final step. We are going to go over your three most important goals so many times that you simply can't do anything but start out fully motivated and take massive action on your goals. Rest assured, I won't bother you with the usual goal formulas or torture you to mess around with the details until you've lost the desire to start working on it. No, instead I would like to introduce you to my tried and true goal-quick-check, which has served me well for quite some years now. It is fast, reliable and provides the necessary clarity.

To put your three most important goals to the test, you only need to ask yourself one single question: "Are my goals S.E.C.S.I.?"

S.E.C.S.I. is an acronym, in which every letter stands for an important quality, which powerful goals should have in my opinion.

Goals have to be S.E.C.S.I.

S for SPECIFIC

Your goal should be as detailed and specific as possible. Vague wishes or "wishy-washy" plans have no place in this stage of the process.

E for EMOTIONAL

Imagine you have already achieved your goal. What happens inside of you? Does the thought of it leave you cold? Then your goal isn't emotional enough. But if you are hit by a wave of intense emotions, you will start making it a reality all on your own. The question you should ask yourself for every goal is the following: "Do I want to achieve that goal with all my heart and my soul?"

C like Concrete

Do you have interim steps, milestones and a deadline that can be measured?

S like SELF-SUFFICIENT

This point is especially important. Can you reach your goal on your own, or do you need the help of others? An example: "I would like to be promoted to branch manager in the upcoming year," is a goal that wouldn't be enough for these criteria, because you would be subject to the behavior of your higher ups. A fitting alternative would be, "I will complete my work motivated and enjoy it in the upcoming year and attach great importance to my results, so my supervisors won't pass me up when the next promotion comes up."

I like INITIATIVE

Last but not least, is your goal motivating enough that you are willing to make a decision and start by yourself?

If you've reviewed the three most important goals according to the *S.E.C.S.I. Formula*, the chances are pretty good that you can hardly wait to get started. But the bigger your plans are the more life will test you on how serious you are. And by overcoming these inevitable obstacles, the fourth pillar of lasting changes will be some help to you.

Use the One Percent Formula

During carnival season, my daughter Emma came home from school and announced excitedly, "Daddy, we were talking about fasting today at school. It was super interesting, and I've decided that I'm going to start fasting too. In particular, I will be doing a sweets-fasting for the next two weeks, because I know they are not good for my teeth and my health." You can't imagine how proud I was, and because I admired her determination, I congratulated her on this decision. All the more surprising it was to me that I saw her sitting at our kitchen table the next day, enjoying a big and tasty Magnum ice cream bar. Because of her spirited announcement the day before, I was a bit surprised but didn't say anything and just sat down next to her. After she had licked every last bit of ice cream off the stick, she happily looked at me and said, "I've realized something, Daddy. You know that I'm currently doing a sweets-fasting. But if I already start making an exception on the first day, I really have a problem."

She was right, because the sweets-fasting was never quite put into practice. And even though I had a big smile in my face at that moment, I had to think about how many people are acting according to this pattern. They announce a desired change with big words, throw themselves more or less enthusiastically into the task, and then give up after a short period of time. But this initial momentum is particularly crucial. Even though having a clear focus, courageous ideas and being highly motivated are very important factors, taking action makes all the difference at the end of the day. Thus, the fourth pillar of lasting changes is a combination of discipline, endurance and the unshakable belief that you can do it.

The more unfamiliar a new thinking or behavior pattern is for us the higher the risk that we fall back into our old habits, simply because it's more convenient. Saying *Oh Yeah!* to change, making an irrevocable decision, as well as having a clear goal will make it indeed very likely that you can face this risk successfully. But you should still, as often as you can, consciously remind yourself that you cannot give up and have to stay on the ball during the first weeks of making a change. Always remember one thing. It's never...

> Success is the combination of discipline, endurance and the unshakable belief that you can do it.

- Easy
- The right time
- Perfect
- The right circumstances
- Guaranteed that you will be successful

Life will make you many unethical offers. It will encourage you to stay in your cozy comfort zone. There are always...

- Reasons not to follow through
- Important other engagements
- Other people who want to change your mind
- Days when you don't feel great
- Situations that you aren't prepared for
- Obstacles in your way
- Doubts about whether you are doing the right thing
- External circumstances working against you
- Sleepless nights
- Long days in the office
- Times when you have to get up early
- Moments when you are afraid

It always seems to be easier to…

- Not do it at all
- Leave everything as it was
- Sit on the couch and watch TV
- Come to terms with the circumstances
- Resign yourself to inertia
- Blame others
- Look for excuses and reasons why things can't work out
- Give up
- Meet the expectations of others, instead of following your own vision

You should expect to have these or similar thoughts running through your mind when you start realizing your goals. If everything goes smoothly and without any obstacles at all, there is a high probability that your goal just isn't big enough. Whether we like it or not, life is not all guns and roses. It's hard, you won't get anything for free, and you will have to start anew every single day. Success, a self-determined life and a general feeling of satisfaction don't just fall from the sky. But if you integrate this *Think it. Do it. Change it.* mentality into your life, the chances are good that nothing can stop you and you will start out happily. And this is exactly why you never need…

- A title, money or the permission of others
- The perfect business plan
- Step-by-step instructions that include every possibility
- A result that's a hundred percent perfect
- The fastest car
- The biggest office
- The newest technical equipment

Just get started. Just do it. Follow your heart and use your mind. You will soon understand that the first miles are the hardest. But with every single day in which you integrate this new behavior into your life, it gets easier.

Last year, I visited the Kennedy Space Center in Cape Canaveral during our family vacation in Florida. One piece of information the guide gave us stuck with me; a space shuttle uses more fuel in the first miles after takeoff than it does during the entire orbit of the earth. Changes are also hard in the beginning and require a lot of strength. But the effort is worth it because your new behavior will eventually become a motivational habit, which brings you closer to your goal, step-by-step. I'm a big proponent of the *One Percent Formula*. I first read about it in a book from Dr. Alan Weiss, and it summarizes the last few paragraphs pretty well:

> *If you improve just one percent every day, you're twice as good in seventy days.*

This statement shows that it's the sum of all the small steps that leads you to success in the end. One of my mentors summarized this, at the very beginning of my career, in a sentence that I haven't forgotten to this day. "Ilja, whenever you are faced with a change in the future, I want you to think in small steps. No matter how small the steps might seem, every single one of them brings you closer to your goal. And before you know it, these many small changes will make a huge difference."

What difference do you want to make? Which new habits do you need to bring yourself and your company to the next level? Whatever your answer may be, I would like to remind you that it is perfectly okay to...

> Changes are also hard in the beginning and require a lot of strength. But the effort is worth it.

- Not know everything ahead of time
- Not have all the answers (no matter what you are told, nobody does!)
- Have a queasy feeling in your stomach sometimes
- Start out imperfect and start learning on the way, due to experiences
- Fall on your face sometimes
- Be satisfied with eighty percent at times (instead of forever waiting for perfection)

All of this is perfectly okay. All that matters is that you get started. On the other hand, it is absolutely not okay...

- To expect everything to go smoothly and work on its own
- To quit right away, if something doesn't go as you imagined
- To expect immediate success and results
- To change nothing and still expect that something will change
- To complain about life, your circumstances, your colleagues or your boss, without making a change
- To constantly ask yourself, *What if?* without ever giving it a try
- To give up your dreams and visions for the expectations of other people

Just give your best and get started! One of my mantras goes like this: "You prepare. You show up. You give it your best shot!" If you act according to this maxim, success will arrive. Start acting and getting things done.

Always make sure that you go your own way, not that of others. It might be rocky at times and you will have to move many obstacles out of your way. You will make mistakes, the more the better because you will learn from them. The important thing is: Get up one more time than you fall down. Admittedly, sometimes you will also need a little bit of luck. I know that you've read many books that said success can be planned on a drawing board. But life, unfortunately, never goes according to plans. And definitely not according to the one we have thought up ourselves. Oftentimes you just need that extra little bit of luck. You have to be at the right place, at the right time, to meet the right person there. But I am firmly convinced that you can also force your luck. The more the correct preparation meets determined action the more you will find yourself in situations that your environment would most likely consider a lucky coincidence.

Chapter Summary

> *Think it. Do it. Change it.* The big ideas of this chapter
>
> ✓ Listen to your heart, but never forget about your mind
> ✓ Nothing is as powerful as a combination of rational analysis and emotionally-driven actions

- ✓ An expert is someone who knows the basics by heart
- ✓ Your money, your energy and your time will go to the areas in life that are important to you
- ✓ Say *Oh Yeah!* as often as you can to change, to transformation, to life
- ✓ A decision for something means a decision against something at the same time
- ✓ Making a real decision means committing to this action with every fiber of your being and not letting yourself be led astray by setbacks
- ✓ Every change starts with an irrevocable decision
- ✓ Use the *S.E.C.S.I. Formula* for successful definition of goals
- ✓ Use the *One Percent Formula* for lasting habits
- ✓ Whatever you do: Be prepared. Show up. Give it your best shot.

The Purpose of Life Is to Live It -
Why New York Is Sometimes Right around the Corner

"Oh oh, come take my hand, we're riding out tonight to case the Promised Land. Oh oh oh, thunder road, oh thunder road, thunder road."

- Bruce Springsteen, Thunder Road

I don't know about you, my dear readers, but I think it is sad and wonderful at the same time that we have reached the last chapter of this book. Sad because our time together is slowly coming to an end (at least for the moment, I would love to meet you all in person one day), but still wonderful because we have passed through so many valleys and climbed so many summits.

It would make me immensely happy if you have said the phrase, "I'm just going to do it!" more than once by this point, and have started to live your life self-determined and with a high inner motivation. Nothing would make me happier than the largest possible number of successes that you have been able to celebrate in various areas of your life because of this book. And if you aren't quite at this point, that's okay too; after all, life is not a picnic, and everyone starts out small. But definitely stay with it. If you commit to your dreams, work hard and never give up, your success will come. Maybe not today or tomorrow, but it will come.

At the same time, I would like to mention the danger associated with this, because nothing slows down as much as success does. "Wait a minute," you will probably object, "I've always thought success is a good thing!" It is, but we always have to be on the alert so that it doesn't make us too comfortable, As Marshall Goldsmith realized in his bestseller with the same title, "What got you here won't get you there." In other words, being successful today means one thing first and foremost: Knowing what worked yesterday.

I often come across the results of such comfort in success during my seminars. On the last day, I always like to hold a quick feedback round and ask my participants what has changed or happened for them during our time together. I admit I have to hold back the tears sometimes, because there are people who literally change their life from the inside out during the short time I am privileged enough to walk alongside them. But there are also the other categories. And I usually hear some sort of variation of the following statement from them: "It was really good. Even though I already knew everything, it felt good to be reassured again."

Statements like this always break my heart, because an attitude like this means certain death for any development as no more growth is happening. Instead, you keep telling yourself that you are already successful and arrange yourself with the status quo. And I really don't want to make a plea for the popular *faster-higher-further* mentality at this point, because, for me, acknowledging even minor details, enjoying moments of peace and being thankful for everything you have are important parts of having a fulfilled life. But I am convinced that we should never rest on the results of the past. Thankfully, the *Think it. Do it. Change it.* mentality is almost forcing you to take the various opportunities that present themselves to you.

Thus, I would like to incite you to stay critical and hungry, even in the moments of great success. Think outside the box, break the rules and keep questioning the supposedly normal circumstances. Be open to innovative ideas and set out on a new path. The mantra is, "Get out of your comfort zone and embrace change". And for this, you will need a good amount of courage, because new ideas are often laughed at that first, and sometimes even strongly fought. This always

> Become a critical thinker, rule breaker and game changer.

makes me angry, because, by now, you know the quote by Niels Bohr that I like to mention so often: "Predictions are difficult, especially if they have to do with the future."

Still, many people react almost automatically with rejection when it comes to new ideas and changing their thinking, because the convenience of the already achieved has become too powerful. They will say things like, "I know all about it," "Already tried that," "This will never work," "Why should I change anything?" or the notorious, "We've always done it this way." Heard that before? Said it before yourself? If this is familiar to you, then rest easy, you aren't the only one. I would like to give you a few prominent examples in history, where innovative people had to fight against a lot of resistance, when they introduced their courageous ideas to the public.

- A driller in 1859 said this, before the very first oil-drilling project: "Drilling for oil? You mean, drilling a hole into the ground and trying to find oil? You must have gone mad!"
- Charles H. Duell, director of the US patent office, made this bold statement in 1899: "Everything that can be invented has already been invented!"
- After German Kaiser Wilhelm II. listened to developer Wilhelm Maybach explain the ten minute long starting procedure of the Mercedes Simplex motor in 1903, he remarked, "The car has no future. I'm putting my money on the horse."
- After being asked about the newest development of sound film in 1927, the film giant Harry Warner was wondering, "Who the hell wants to hear actors talk?"
- The boss of 20th Century Fox, Darryl F. Zanuck, predicted in 1946, "The TV won't prevail on the market. People will soon get tired of having to look at a plywood box every night." (An almost visionary prognosis, because most people today are already sitting in front of the TV at noon or in the mornings.)
- When the Beatles sent their demo tape to Decca Recordings in 1962, their rejection letter read, "We don't like your sound. And groups of guitars are on their way out anyway."
- And in 1995 Microsoft Boss Bill Gates dared to make my absolute favorite prediction: "The internet is just a hype."

And now imagine if all the people who had these phenomenal ideas had listened to the critics, the complainers and the know-it-alls and said, "Okay, I really don't know if this is going to work out. I'd better give up now." But no, thankfully they believed in their ideas and fought for their dreams. And we can take something away from this for our daily lives. Every change is hard in the beginning. When something is new, it's perfectly normal to be unsure and have doubts about whether it is the right thing to do. But if you actively want to create change, you just have to dare to become a critical thinker, rule breaker and game changer. The reason is simple. The world doesn't care whether you change or not. But one thing you can be sure of; society, your customers and the people around you definitely do.

As it happens, life is oftentimes the best teacher. Recently, I was giving a guest lecture about change management at a university in Berlin. And as I was looking into the faces of the students, one thing became very apparent to me. Even though I would consider myself pretty innovative and open at 40 years old, I already belong to the "old school" generation. Even my daughter Emma asked me the other day, "Daddy, how does it feel to be that old?" And I had to think about that exact question in that moment at the university, because the students in the auditorium were on average twenty-one years old, which means born in 1994 (do you remember what you did in 1994?). Please let these numbers sink in for a moment, because that means:

- These young people were born five years after the fall of the Berlin Wall and never experienced the GDR (German Democratic Republic, aka East Germany).
- Helmut Kohl is a guy they probably never heard of, and for them it's hard to imagine that Germany once had a chancellor that wasn't a woman (think Angela Merkel).
- They have never used music cassettes, telephones with a wire or a telex machine (and probably also don't know what a fax is, either). Even the CD player and the first iPod models are more or less antique relics rather than achievements of modern technology.
- They don't know Back to the future with Michael J. Fox, Knight Rider with David Hasselhoff, or the original cast of Star Trek. They've never in their lives used a TV that only had seven channels, where you had to get up from the couch in order to switch programs—only to see everything in black and white.
- Instead, every single one of them owns at least an iPad, iPhone and a laptop (probably an Apple Watch, too), communicates through

Facebook messenger, Instagram or WhatsApp eighty percent of the time, and is online 24/7.

And here's my point. At the very latest, in five years, these young people will be your customers, co-workers and some cases maybe even your bosses. Which brings us to the moment of truth. Do you think this is a great thing, or does this scare you? In the end it doesn't matter, regardless of how you rate it, because it is what it is. Neither you nor I will be able to stop this development (and you can expect to be experiencing another set of innovations in the next few years).

> The better you are prepared for future trends the better you are able to deal with them.

But the better prepared you are for these futures trends, the more successful you will be. And it gets even easier if you become a trendsetter yourself, if you do your own thing, regardless of external circumstances, trends and influences. This brings us to the main subject of this chapter, the more you do your own thing the more purposeful your life will be. And the more purpose you put into every single moment the more intense your daily experiences get. The more exciting things you experience the more naturally you will be able to handle the different developments in your future. If you're asking yourself now, *This all sounds good and well, but how do I give my life a purpose?* then I would like to give you two answers. The ultra short version is the purpose of life is to live it (this, by the way, is a sentence that's worth thinking about it a bit more). The longer variation goes as follows: The biggest motivation and the deepest purpose can be found in achieving. In doing, implementing and taking action. In order to give you the really detailed version, I have to share some background information with you.

The New-York-Quick-Check for Lasting Changes

For over twenty years, I have been a huge fan of singer and songwriter Udo Jürgens. Born in a small Austrian village, he became an international star who played concerts all over the world, sold over a hundred million records during his career and composed songs for Shirley Bassey, Sammy Davis jr. and Frank Sinatra. And even if he died of a heart attack at the age of eighty, two years ago, the music of Udo Jürgens will live with us forever. I've always been fascinated by the life story of this terrific artist, because he was the perfect example of how the life of a Changemaker can look put into practice. But even more, I like his songs, lyrics and melodies because they have accompanied me during different phases in my life. They have inspired, helped and motivated me.

But it doesn't stop here because, for over twelve years now, I have been playing my absolute favorite song from Udo Jürgens at the beginning, in the breaks and at the end of my seminars, trainings and workshops. It's called, "Ich war noch niemals in New York" (I've never been to New York). I love that song, and especially the lyrics, because it's like an anthem that represents the desire for change. And my participants, well, if you hear that song five times a week, seven times a time, it always has an impact on you. Because that song had been a companion for so long, one day I had a crazy idea. *Why not hold an entire seminar in New York one day?* And I was so obsessed with that vision that, one year later, together with a group of twenty people, I was flying to the Big Apple for a change seminar.

Part of the program was a challenge designed to stretch the comfort zone. And it went something like this. The participants were instructed to spread out to famous hot spots like the *Statue of Liberty, Central Park,* or *Brooklyn Bridge* and find a group of at least fifteen New Yorkers and teach them to sing the song that brought us there, "I have never been to New York". Not in English, but in German. So for the whole day everybody was entirely focused on Udo Jürgens and his great song. At many places in New York it was sung by people from all over the world and you could say that the spirit of Udo Jürgens was blowing through New York that day.

Meanwhile, I was walking more or less aimlessly through Manhattan, cherishing the unique atmosphere of the city. I was thinking about my participants a lot, humming the melody of the song, and mentally asked myself if Udo Jürgens already had the hiccups from so many people thinking about him right now. But what happened next still surprises me to this day.

May I ask you if you believe in such things as coincidences or fate? I would like to share a short statistic with you. There are more than eight million people living in Manhattan alone. Add about five million commuters and tourists, so we are talking about a total of about thirteen million people who happened to be in New York on this particular day at this particular time. Please keep this in the back of your mind, because here is what happened.

I was walking from Madison Avenue towards Central Park when I had to stop at a red light. While I was waiting for it to turn green, I noticed a man on the other side of the street who looked very familiar. I really had to look back at him a few times until I was absolutely certain. Who was standing on the other side of the street, on that special day in New York? Exactly. It was him. Udo Jürgens was standing in front of me, in living color.

And I noticed instinctively that this was a once-in-a-lifetime chance. So I put on my nicest smile and said, "Hello Udo." Of course, I told him what my participants were currently doing in the city, why his song meant so much to me, and how many people were currently singing it in different areas of New York. And do you want to know what Udo Jürgens said to me right off the bat? I can't even remember. But I will never forget how I felt back then. This successful international star made me feel like I was the most important person to him in that moment on Madison Avenue.

All in all, we chatted for a few minutes, and, at the end, I asked him a question that had been running through my mind a lot during this time. "I know so many people that are already frustrated at the age of twenty or thirty. What is your secret, how do you manage to still do what you do with so much passion and motivation at almost eighty years old?" And I'm still fascinated to this day with the answer Udo Jürgens gave me. He thought about it for a moment and then he said, "That's simple, you just have to find your personal New York in life. And then you do everything it takes to get there."

I still get goose bumps when I think about that moment because this simple piece of advice applies to every kind of change, to the big ones as well the as small ones, to the easy ones and the hard ones. Nothing works when you put your emergency brake on, you can't change even a bit that way. It's either all or nothing. And isn't that what life is all about? When you know what and why you want to change, you will find a way, because you are

> Find your personal New York in life. And then do everything it takes to get there.

willing to make mistakes and to learn from the failures that definitely will happen. And I am convinced that I can comprehend the reason behind this statement from Udo Jürgens so well because I know what great effects it can have when you set out on the path to your own personal New York, judging by my own story.

As you read in the beginning of the book (hopefully, you did not skip the *About the Author* section), I have been a department store manager for various retail companies such as Karstadt, Hertie, Wertheim and IKEA. For seven years I was in charge of a total of ten different stores all over Germany. During that time, I had to fight with various types of change almost daily, personally as well as with my team. And I don't exactly remember when it came down to it, but, at one point, the subject of how to successfully deal with change wasn't letting me go. You could almost say I was obsessed with it. This fascination then almost inevitably turned into a dream. I wanted to start my own business; I wanted to write books and give keynote speeches. But as my dream grew, so did my fear of the necessary change.

I will never forget the day when my life was completely turned upside down. It was March 8th, 2008 and, from the outside looking in, I had reached the height of my career, but on the inside I had reached rock bottom. I was frustrated, feeling other-directed and never saw my family because I was working in Hamburg and our home base was in Berlin. I definitely hadn't imagined my life like this, but I hadn't quite found the courage to change anything yet. But, one day, as I was stuck in a traffic jam on the highway, an eye-opening realization hit me: "Nobody is forcing me to keep on doing what I'm doing. I can make the decision any time to switch course and do what I want to do, instead." This unknown clarity hit me so hard that I just couldn't help but say, "I'm just going to do it!" consciously for the very first time.

What happened afterwards is history, as they say. I made the decision to quit my career in retail and follow my calling as a keynote speaker, change coach and author. And I know this all sounds pretty smooth and simple in hindsight, but it definitely wasn't. The price of my decision was huge because I had to start from scratch on a lot of levels. My colleagues and acquaintances just shook their heads in disbelief back then. They said, "How can you just give up such a well-paid and secure job?" In addition to this, I had just built a house and my older daughter had just turned two years old. This made the emotional pressure even stronger, because they accused me of acting completely irresponsibly.

But I am sure that this was the very reason I became successful, because the emotional drive was so strong, because I wanted nothing more than to successfully implement this change, because my family was my new team.

They were always the only ones that I could rely on one hundred percent when it came to my plans and now it was their turn to be able to rely on me. And you know what? Since the moment when I made my decision in the traffic jam, I haven't had to worry about my motivation again. Since that day, I know what I do it for, *why* I do it. Because I have found my personal New York in life. It's right around the corner in Berlin Pankow. But most of all, because I am willing to do everything it takes to get exactly there.

And I would like to ask you a few questions now that have hopefully crossed your mind already while reading. "What does your personal New York in life look like? What makes you jump out of bed energetically in the morning? Which subject are you so positively obsessed with that you cannot let it go?" The more you want to change yourself with all your heart and soul and have the support of a strong team the more successful you will be able to handle upcoming challenges.

Are you not quite sure yet? Then I would like to introduce you to a powerful technique that I've been using for years, that will either help you uncover your personal New York in life or strengthen it once more. I call it the *New-York- Quick-Check* for Lasting Changes. And it goes like this. In order to truly keep working on my motivation, I ask myself three questions that have a very powerful effect, every day, the first one in the morning, right after waking up, and the others in the evening when I review the events of the day in my head.

The New-York-Quick-Check for Lasting Changes

- Question 1: Which three things do I definitely want to accomplish today?
- Question 2: Which five things that I have experienced today am I especially grateful for?
- Question 3: Have I gotten closer to my personal New York in Life with my ideas, decisions and actions?

My challenge to you: Try this for at least four weeks, longer if you'd like, but definitely not any shorter. (If you need a motivational companion by your side for an entire year, I highly recommend using my change journal, which I published last year.) Of course, I am well aware that only a small portion of my readers will take this challenge. But if you pull through with the *New-York-Quick-Check*, you will realize how much your focus will change, how much you will recognize what really counts in life and how much bigger and more powerful your personal motivation gets. Maybe you will also find out that you don't even have to cross the Atlantic Ocean to find your personal New York; it's right around the corner—deep within you.

> What makes you jump out of bed energetically in the morning? Which subject are you so positively obsessed with that you cannot let it go?

One Hour Makes the Difference

Are you one of those people who like to compare themselves to others? Your best friend is more successful at his job, your neighbor drives a faster car and all of your role models are out of your league in any case. The problem with these kinds of comparisons is that they lead to a completely distorted view of the world because, unfortunately, we tend to either compare ourselves to people who already are where we have wanted to get for years, or with those who we surpassed a while ago when it comes to our personal development.

When it comes to comparisons like these, you can't possibly win. Imagine you are a mediocre golf player and have decided to work on your handicap for the next twelve months. No matter how big your progress may be, if you compare your actual skills with those of Jason Spieth, this will inevitably lead to frustration, dissatisfaction and low self-esteem. If you use an absolute beginner as your reference point instead, the result is a combination of laziness, false satisfaction and backward development.

So just forgo these comparisons from the start, they do not do you any good anyway. Instead, I would recommend you be happy for others in times of success, learn from them and then solely focus on your own development. The only person you should compare yourself with is you. What kind of hidden potential do you have? What are you capable of? What can you achieve when you disengage all the parking breaks? Only when you make the best possible version of yourself your reference point can you set out on your path to unfold your full potential in all areas of your life. And depending which level you are currently on, this can't happen from one day to the next. But you can achieve it if you are willing to work hard for your personal New York in life, make mistakes along the way and then learn from them.

The important thing is to make this mentality a daily habit, this happens faster than you may think sometimes. When I was a store manager at IKEA, we experienced a shortage off staff in the receiving department one summer. To show that we walked our talk about team spirit, we, as a management board, decided to jump in for a week so the staff could still take their planned vacations. What did this mean for me? Getting up at three o'clock in the morning, starting work at three-thirty, and then putting away goods for eight hours so the customers weren't standing in front of empty shelves when the store opened.

One night, I was assigned to the home textiles department and was standing in front of a huge pallet full of boxes that were waiting to be unpacked and then sorted onto each shelf. In the first box was a very special product, a sheepskin called *Ludde*. If you don't know it, it's one of those classic things that you put either in front of your bed or in front of your fireplace. Most importantly, it's one of IKEA's best sellers.

Up until this point, I had always assumed that the sheepskin *Ludde* was made from synthetic fur. But right when I opened the first box just a little crack, I realized that this assumption was very wrong. Because as soon as I put down the Xacto knife, a terrible smell that can only be described as, "Phew, sheep!" hit me. If you're just innocently reading this, admittedly, it might not sound that bad, but in this special moment I felt like I was going to pass out. But as a leader, you have to deal with this, so I bravely sorted about twenty furs onto their shelves.

I was just about to treat myself to a coffee as a reward, when my gaze hit the pallet. And what did I see? Another nine boxes full of sheepskin *Ludde*. Nine more repetitions of this foul stench. But then something remarkable happened. When I got to the second box, I had to force myself to even open it. It was still pretty hard when it came to the third one. Once I got to the fourth box, it wasn't quite as bad. And when I opened the fifth, I thought, *Well, sheep really don't smell THAT bad.* It kept getting more and more normal as I opened the sixth, seventh and eight box. And after I had put the ninth box away, I actually had this thought: *I think I am going to buy me a sheepskin Ludde for myself, and put it in front of the fireplace at home!*

I find it remarkable how fast we get used to a certain way of thinking and acting. And once these things are in place, it's pretty hard to get rid of them again. If you've ever tried to replace an old habit with a new one before, you know exactly what I mean. The cozy comfort zone says hello, because we like to defend nothing more that our beloved routines. So it would be pretty useful if we could acquire a few strong habits for success. How do you like the thought of your ideas, decisions and actions supporting you, instead of holding you back? If you were so good in an area of your life that you are regarded as a sought-after expert by your environment? The good news is: This is possible. The bad news: It takes a lot of commitment, stamina and the unconditional desire to make your personal New York a reality.

> Become an expert in one special area of life.

As always, it starts with a decision. Who do you want to be, what do you want to achieve and which area do you want to be an expert in? Let's imagine you want to become a successful entrepreneur. Then the most important thing is to acquire the corresponding mindset, the necessary knowledge and the required skills. Depending on where you stand today, it should be clear that such a development doesn't happen from one day to the next. Especially not if you are currently still working at an office job that you have to devote eight to ten hours a day to.

But how long does it take exactly, until you become a true expert? Malcolm Gladwell has figured out an easy to remember rule of thumb in his book *Outliers – The Story of Success*. "In fact, researchers have settled on what they believe is the magic number for true expertise: ten thousand hours." Of course, talent always plays a certain role as well, but, in conclusion, this rule of thumb coincides with the experiences I made in my own life, and the life of hundreds of businessmen, executives and managers.

So let's do the math. A year consists of exactly 8.760 hours. If you weren't doing anything but work on the subject of entrepreneurship, you would reach your goal in a little more than a year. But you still have to sleep, have a family, a job, hobbies, friends and other obligations. You'll quickly realize that 10.000 hours can be quite a lot. But please do not give up before you even get started.

My contention is that you can still become a master of your trade, if you have a fulltime job, a family and obligations. All you need is one hour a day. Sixty minutes. 3.600 seconds. During this time, don't do anything else. Just commit yourself completely to studying your subject of choice. "But, Ilja, where am I going to find a whole hour in my schedule? It's just not possible!" Trust me, if your personal New York is big enough, if you really want to achieve it with every fiber of your being, then you will find a way to free those sixty minutes. It's all a question of priorities. If you need a few ideas, cut out evening television, the countless Facebook visits or the never-ending game of Candy Crush on your smartphone. When you start weeding through your day to cut out unproductive time wasters, you will find a ton of other possibilities. And we are now going to take a look at what to use that time you just found for.

The Four Stages of Learning

If you decide to get up an hour earlier, take some time out in the middle of your day or work extra shifts for your personal New York after the day is done, the important thing is that you say to yourself, *I'm just going to do it!* and then get started. To get back to our example, take one hour to do nothing but commit yourself to the subject of entrepreneurship, without distractions, but with one hundred percent focus. Many people do not have the slightest clue how much they can get done in a single hour. For example, you could...

- Study a textbook
- Get inspired by the biographies of successful entrepreneurs
- Watch DVDs or online courses
- Work on your technical skills
- Read blog posts, scientific papers or newsletters about the subject
- Talk to like-minded people about the subject
- Write down your ideas, thoughts and plans in your change journal
- Make a business plan

And so on. The possibilities are truly endless. The more you immerse yourself in the subject the better you will get. The result: Your motivation inevitably rises and your focus starts to shift. You start getting things done, and, through that, you give your life a purpose. Before you know it, you've completed the four stages of learning and are considered a true expert. What, you have never heard of this model of a learning curve? Then I would like to introduce you to it, because every possible development takes place according to this pattern.

Learning stage one: Subconscious incompetence

This stage applies to most people in most subject areas. There is just too much knowledge and too much information in the world, so it is simply not possible to take it all in at once. For this reason, even the smartest people have blind spots and there is a lot that they don't know or cannot do. But because they never dealt with it, they aren't aware of this.

In learning stage one, you are clueless.

Learning stage 2: Conscious incompetence

The more you start doing things the more you take advantage of the many possibilities that life has to offer. And suddenly you come across a subject that is completely new to you. You take an interest in art, music, sports or entrepreneurship and suddenly you find yourself in learning stage two and have opened the gates to a whole new world. There still is a lot that you don't know about and cannot do, but by now you are well aware of this fact. To say it like Socrates, "I know that I know nothing."

In learning stage two, you are a beginner.

Learning stage three: Conscious competence

It get's exciting in stage three. The more you occupy yourself with a subject the more knowledge, ability and information you absorb, just like the proverbial sponge, until you are also able to use it practically. But your new skills are still pretty new, so that you have to consciously remind yourself how to do it with every single step you take. That's why a beginning golfer practices the movements of the backswing and follow through, the piano player the position of his hands and the entrepreneur the basics of bookkeeping and sales.

It's a little bit like your first driving lesson. You have to think about what feels like a thousand things at the same time. The gas pedal is on the right and the brake on the left. Don't forget to buckle up and look behind you. The mirrors need adjusting and the parking break needs to be released. The radio is playing and all the while the driving teacher is asking more or less practical questions. And after you've paid attention to it all, you gas it and stall the engine after a fast-paced drive of a few feet at 5mph. At least that's how it went for me.

In learning stage three, you are a layman.

Learning stage four: Subconscious competence

Let's stick with the example of driving. As time went on, your skills improved and, over the years, you have been driving tens of thousands of miles on the roads of this world. Eventually, you've reached the point where you really don't have to think about each procedure. And since then, it's all been happening subconsciously. Your hands and feet switch gears automatically, additionally, you can make a phone call, write a text message or talk to your passenger. At the same time, your kids ask you for the tenth time, "Are we there yet?" All the while you are listening to the nice voice on the radio. In this case, you have reached the level of subconscious competence, and it starts being a lot of fun.

In learning stage four, you are an expert.

No matter what subject you deal with, as time goes by, you go through all four stages of learning. And if you are truly committed, it won't take an eternity. Of course, nobody can walk these miles for you, make the necessary mistakes and learn from them. But even if you just spend one hour a day working on your chosen subject area, this makes seven hours a week, thirty a month, and 360 a year. And then another connection plays into your hands. The better you get, and the more experiences you have, the more time you will want to put into your personal New York. Soon, that one hour a day is going to turn into two, and even more after a certain amount of time. Before you know it, you've become really good and finally find yourself at the level of subconscious competence. You have reached expert status.

Of course, this takes some time, but not forever. You don't need the full 10.000 hours to be really good at your subject. In my opinion, half of it is enough to be better than eighty percent of your competitors. An hour a day can make all the difference in the world. The important thing is that you start doing it. No matter where you are today, if you want to invest an hour or half a day into your plans, every single minute counts. When you look back in a year, you will wish that you had gotten started today. The philosophy is simple. Do your best every day and try to become a little bit better than you were yesterday. The rest happens naturally on the way if you are serious about it.

If you are really convinced that you are serious, I would like to invite you to critically question this attitude as often as you can because we can always go the extra mile and give just a little bit more than is expected. I would like to tell you about an encounter that really shaped me in regards to this. A few years ago, I had the opportunity to meet a very impressive entrepreneur. When I asked him about his hobbies, he answered, "I don't have any hobbies. When I do something, I do it right. No matter what it is." This mindset is exactly what you need because, if you don't do it, nobody will do it for you. You have to make the decision, walk the miles and keep going, even when life is testing how serious you are, once again.

> Go all out, or do not do anything at all. No half measures.

When it comes to a transforming *Think it. Do it. Change it.* mentality in its purest form, there probably isn't a better role model than Arnold Schwarzenegger, who recently posted a video on Instagram where he made the following statement: "When I see guys texting in the gym, they're not serious. This is Mickey Mouse stuff. You train or you don't. In Germany, we say: Wenn schon, denn schon. If you do it then do it. Go all out!" There is nothing more to be said. When you do something, go all out or don't do it at all—in every single area of your life.

Fire the Whiners, Know-it-alls and Grouches

Some time ago, union strikes were happening repeatedly in Berlin schools and kindergartens, so I was lucky enough to spend a whole day with my two daughters. After we did some crafts and played for a while, Emma and Elisabeth got hungry, so they communicated loud and clear that they desired a solid meal. And, of course, the well-being of my two princesses is dearer to my heart than anything else, so I did what every caring father would have done in my situation. We drove straight to McDonald's.

But before we were able to take a bite of our juicy burgers, we had to do one thing: Wait. Because right in front of us in line was a man who had ordered two Big Mac meals. It was a standard order, so the cashier was going through the standard motions and asked, "Do you want fries and ketchup with that?"

The man answered, "Yes please."

And on it went, "Coke or Fanta?"

And then a disturbance happened in the standard procedure, because the answer was, "No, thank you, I don't want anything to drink."

The cashier didn't quite expect that, because he said, "But the drinks are included in the meal."

The man answered, "I know that, but I still don't want anything to drink."

"But that would be stupid, you're paying for the drinks after all."

"I know, but I still don't want them."

Now the cashier started to get panicky, "But you can't do that."

And the man asked, "Why not?"

"Because I can't sell you the meal without a drink. You have to order one." And it went on like a game of ping-pong.

The man said, "But I don't want one."

"Then I can't sell you the meal."

"But I'm not thirsty."

"I'm sorry, but you have to order one."

Finally, the man said what I would have probably said two minutes ago. "Can I please have a word with your manager?"

So the cashier went in the back and the manager appeared—a young girl, maybe twenty-two years old, with freckles on her face and piercings in her nose, lip and both eyebrows. And she said, slightly annoyed, "I hear there's a problem with the drinks?"

By now, the whole line was curious how this was all going to end. And the man desperately explained. "Not really, I just don't want anything to drink."

To this the manager replied, "But you have to order a drink, or else we can't sell you the meals."

And the whole spiel started anew. But after a few rounds of argument ping-pong, the mood in the restaurant started to shift. It got louder. The first people waiting took off, and a murmur went through the crowd until a little boy in the back of the line yelled, "Hey, if the man orders two cokes, and I drink them, can we finally move on?"

If you had been there, you would have felt how much relief overcame multiple people—the man, because he finally got his food, the people in line, because the waiting was over, and especially the manager and her cashier, because now they could enter both drinks into their cash register with great satisfaction.

I was not quite sure if I should laugh or cry at that moment. But most of all, I was asking myself a crucial question: Was this an exception? I don't think it was, for more reasons than one. How many times do we do things only because we've always done them a certain way? How many times are the company policies more important to us than the needs of our customers? How many times do we try to convince the people around us to do something that they really don't want to do? Then we usually say, "You have to do this, you have to stop doing that." And what's the result? Opposition, denial, resistance to change. Those who don't want to change will not change, no matter how much we lure with our carrot or threaten with the stick. One law of change that is written in stone applies here: People only change for reasons that are important to them, and never because of the ones we would like them to do it for.

Thus, as we get to the end of this book, I would like to address a subject that you will inevitably be confronted with when you use the *Think it. Do it. Change it.* mentality on daily basis and set out on the path to your personal New York in life. I'm talking about the ever-increasing resistance to change, the subtle or very open refusal of new ideas, ways and behaviors. Because one thing is as sure as eggs are eggs. Using your full motivation to lead a life that

> Do not waste your energy. People only change for their own reasons.

deserves this name doesn't mean that your environment is going to follow along excitedly. Quite the opposite, chances are good that you will have to deal with the typical whiners, know-it-alls and grouches that try to talk you out of your plans with a rarely displayed energy.

But how does one best react to this kind of resistance? How do you manage to motivate other people to a desired change? You already know, from the motivational chapter, that motivation is one of those things that are not so simple to deal with. It's the easiest thing in the world to discourage people. A single word, a careless decision or a wrong action can manage to make an entire team's motivation drop rapidly. But it is nearly impossible to get someone to move from point A to point B when they do not want to do it. If you've tried to motivate someone in vain before then you will know what I am talking about.

Even if this sounds pretty devastating at first, at the same time there is good news, because it is definitely possible to get our environment excited about change. And it's worth putting a lot of energy and passion into this because nothing is more powerful than the support of a motivated and reliable team. It is as simple as it is effective. If we want others to change, we have to give them a rational and an emotional reason, a powerful vision that makes it worth starting to take action. You know the drill: *Always go first.* Show and lead by example what you want others to do. If you are excited, you will excite others. If you are motivated, you will motivate others. If you change yourself and your way of communicating, the people around you will also change, not because they have to but because they suddenly want to. This means we need the ability to awaken the inner motivation to change in others, to trust them and get them excited about our ideas.

If you communicate a compelling vision and live it with every fiber of your being, most people in your environment will dive into change full of motivation and of their own free will. But at the same time, there will be others who cannot get started and instead just stay in the status quo. And this is for one of two reasons.

- Reason One: Not knowing something or not being able to do something
- Reason Two: Not wanting to do something

As far as the first reason goes, there is a simple solution. Offer your full support so that the desired knowledge, the required abilities and necessary tools can be learned and adapted as quickly as possible. This looks a bit different for the second reason. If someone has all the required prerequisites but simply doesn't want to change, then, unfortunately, you cannot change that fact. I would encourage you to try again, but in most cases it's a waste of time. In this case, there is only one thing you can and should do—ban the complainers, know-it-alls and whiners from your life in a respectful but consequent manner. Fire them. Life is way too short to have your plans badmouthed by these backward thinking, negative and change resistant people.

Who will you pull on your team? Which people are good for you but challenge you at the same time? Either in a business setting or in your personal life, you should spend time on nothing more than putting together your inner circle, because change only happens when you are supporting each other, not if you are working against each other. A properly functioning team pushes, supports and motivates each other, but always offers constructive feedback. This way, all team members grow as individuals, but also as a group, and before you know it, the individual, "I'm just going to do it!" turns into a collective, "We are just going to do it!"

> Every change efforts gets easier when you have the support of a strong team.

You always have the choice of who you want to be a part of your inner circle. I highly recommend you only surround yourself with people who support you on your way to uniqueness. By the way, this doesn't mean you can't criticize each other. Quite the opposite, you can always tell who your good friends are, because they also bring up uncomfortable things. But those who waste all their energy on being destructive and negative definitely shouldn't have a place in your life.

Well, with this we have reached the end of the book. I hope I was able to challenge you more than once and encourage you to keep on doing it. If you found one big idea that was helpful for your current situation in life then I am more than happy. In addition, also let the ideas from this chapter sink in and give your personal New York in life enough time and space. The more powerful your inner drive is the easier it will be to make the *Think it. Do it. Change it.* mentality a vital part of your daily life.

Whatever your plans are for the future, it would make me very happy if, from time to time, you hear my voice in your head, telling you to *Think it. Do it. Change it.* In the moments of doubt and fear, I want you to remember the mantra and say it to yourself: "I'm just going to do it!" And then just go ahead and do it.

This really doesn't require a huge and one-time action, because the many seemingly insignificant details of everyday life are much more important than that. There are conversations, behaviors, and actions that we tend to avoid so gladly, but oftentimes it is these small pieces of the puzzle that make the big difference between success and failure. And this, too, is one of those facts that I have learned from a very special woman. It was an encounter that, most likely, I will not forget for the rest of my life because, even in a flirt in a bar, one simple detail can make all the difference in the world.

A few years ago, I went to a club one evening. While I was waiting for my friend Stefan at the bar, an attractive, young and very blonde woman who was sending me very obvious signals was standing just a few feet away from me. I was already spoken for at that time, and therefore not interested. But talking isn't a crime and that's how it all started. If you had been there, you probably would have described this young lady as a Paris Hilton type, just based on her looks. And after she spoke the initial few sentences, you'd know right away: Definitely not that smart. But she was very appealing, so I asked, "Tell me, what do you do for a living?"

She was still totally in flirt mode and answered, "Well, you're going to have to take an educated guess."

So I played along and said, "Okay, but at least tell me what letter it starts with."

She announced, "It starts with a W."

Well, I had a certain presumption, so I took a shot in the dark, "Hmmm... Are you maybe a women's hairdresser?"

To this she answered, and please let this sink in: "Wrong, I'm a wendor!"

> You decide who is going to be a member of your inner circle. Choose the people wisely.

And I admit this encounter has changed me. And companies, organizations and society as a whole changes when the people change. It always comes down to people, people like you and me, who eventually decide that they won't take it anymore and start making a change. Don't wait any longer. Leave the hesitation to others. Overcome your fears. Instead, announce, "I'm just going to do it!" as often as you can and lead the changes for your personal environment. Others will gladly follow you.

At the end of this book, please imagine that you only have one single task in life, starting today, and that is to influence the people around you with your mentality, your attitude, and your mindset. As soon as you enter a room, everybody aligns himself or herself with you. What would happen to your company, your family and your environment? Would you serve as a good or as a bad example? Would you hold back or would you motivate?

You know what, this really isn't a theoretical consideration at all, because all of us influence the people around us in each encounter, each conversation and in every moment with what we say, what we do and sometimes also with the things we do not do. No matter what point in your life you are at in this moment, what title you have or how much money you make, you are always able to make a difference. You are able to actively initiate change. You are able to influence the people around with your *Think it. Do it. Change it. Mentality.* I wish you the best of luck with this.

Chapter Summary

Think it. Do it. Change it. The big ideas of this chapter

- ✓ Being successful today means knowing what worked well yesterday
- ✓ Stay hungry and critical even in moments of success
- ✓ The better prepared you are for future developments the more successful you will be
- ✓ The biggest motivation and the deepest meaning lie in doing—in achieving, implementing and acting
- ✓ Find your personal New York in life. And then do everything it takes to get there
- ✓ Use the *New-York-Quick-Check* for Lasting Changes to reach your goals
- ✓ Be happy for the success of others and focus on yourself
- ✓ Invest at least one hour a day in your personal development
- ✓ Use the four stages of learning to become an expert in your field
- ✓ Give your best every day and try to be a little bit better than you were yesterday
- ✓ Live according to the principle of *Always Go First!*
- ✓ Fire the complainers, know-it-alls and comfort zone builders out of your daily life, in a respectful but consequent manner
- ✓ Lead the changes and influence the people in your environment

Epilogue: Making History

"Take me out tonight. Where there's music and there's people, who are young and alive. Driving in your car, I never, never want to go home. Because I haven't got one anymore."
                    - The Smiths, There is a light that never goes out

It doesn't take more than forty-five minutes for the sun to go down on the horizon. And it is fascinating to me how fast the atmosphere of a whole city can change in such a short amount of time. Where the water taxis slowly tugged along the Chao Phraya River just a moment ago, jet-set parties are starting on luxury yachts. It is my impression that everyone flooded outside at the same time. The place I am observing this from is the rooftop bar on the 31st floor of the Millennium Hotel in Bangkok. A pleasantly cool wind makes the humidity bearable; there is piano music in the background and, fully relaxed, I'm sipping my Argentinian Malbec. This morning I gave a keynote speech at an international sales conference in front of leaders from all over the world, and now I have some time to let the fascination of the city have its effect on me.

And I don't know if it was this overwhelming moment above the roofs of Bangkok, but suddenly a few questions popped into my head. *What would my life have looked like if I hadn't made that decision to quit my presumably secure job eight years ago? What would have happened if I had allowed the fear of change to paralyze me? Would I be as happy and satisfied as I am today?*

Even though there will never be an answer to these thoughts, I know that I wouldn't exchange the past few years for anything in the world. I am filled with a deep sense of gratitude when I think about all the experiences, encounters, and the ups and downs of this time. And another thing has become very apparent to me. I can only enjoy the autonomy, the intensity and the variety today, because I consciously told myself this sentence in a powerful moment for the very first time in my life: "I'm just going to do it!" These six simple words had the power to turn my entire life upside down, to take me on a roller coaster ride, with twists and turns and speedy descents that got more and more intense. I still have a lot planned and you can look forward to exciting projects from me in the future.

In this book, I was once again privileged enough to share some experiences of my everyday life with you, my dear readers. Oftentimes I am asked, "Ilja, tell me, nothing ever happens to me. Where do you get all your stories? Did you really experience them all or do you make this stuff up?"

This question always surprises me, because life is full of exciting experiences. At your job, with your family, on your commute to work, while shopping and even while visiting the zoo; everywhere you have the opportunity to meet great people and experience great things. Thus, all the stories in my book are taken from my life. Of course, I've often changed people's names for obvious reasons, and I have taken the liberty as a writer to embellish some of the passages, while omitting detail in other areas. All in all, everything happened exactly like this and my reservoir of interesting stories is all but empty. A while ago, I met the green party politician Jürgen Trittin in the sauna, for example, as... Well, you know I'd better tell you this story during one of my speeches or in my next book.

> Just do it. Start making history.

Think about this: The more intense your life gets, the more you will experience stories that are worth telling. But none of this happens on its own. If you passively sit on your couch, and hope that an external event or another person will give you that much needed impulse then you are waiting in vain. Only if you create the change in the next few years actively and are self-determined will you experience all the ups and downs that will result in the corresponding stories. Experience today what you want to talk about tomorrow.

But all this is nothing compared to the most important story of them all—your personal story. Your personality, your experiences and all the miles that you've walked in your life combine to create a unique story that no Hollywood blockbuster movie could hold a candle to. Your task is to develop that uniqueness and to carry it into the world. Believe me; there is no better feeling than proudly announcing, "You know what, I just did it!"

Whenever you feel the impulse to take another step on your journey, I would encourage you to overcome the fear of change and, instead, say, "I'm just going to do it!" with complete conviction. The more stories you write the more you are making history.

Don't wait.

Do it.

Now.

Think it. Do it. Change it.

All the best for your journey.
Ilja Grzeskowitz

P.S: There are two things you could do immediately. If you liked reading the book then I would very much appreciate it if you would write me a review on Amazon. It helps potential readers and you would be supporting me as well. It only takes a minute and it would mean the world to me. Thank you for doing it in advance. And, once again, I'd like to refer to the exclusive Facebook Group, where you can chat with and talk to other readers of this book (including me, of course. BTW, are we friends on FB yet? Let's connect). Just be a part of this community, it will be worth it: https://www.facebook.com/groups/MachEsEinfach/

Acknowledgments

So that was it. My sixth book overall, and—even more exciting—my very first one in English to be published internationally. I can't tell you how proud I am, and I hope that you were able to get a feeling of the passion I tried to put into every single chapter, every single sentence and, yes, every single word. It still feels like a miracle, how a vague idea can finally turn into the book you are holding in your hands right now. But, as always in life, the whole is more than the sum of its parts. Developing, writing and publishing a book is the result of great teamwork. Therefore, I'd like to thank the people who helped me make all of it happen.

Thanks to the whole team at iUniversity for being a great partner. A big shout out also goes to my German publisher, *GABAL*. Together, we already published four books, and it was the whole team around Ursula Rosengart, Ute Flockenhaus and especially André Jünger, who made contact with the guys from iUniverse.

Many thanks to my speakers' bureau *5 Sterne Redner*. The fantastic team around Heinrich Kürzeder not only takes care of my speaking business around the world, but is also a great sparring partner for developing new ideas and projects. You guys rock!

Thank you so much Jeffrey Hayzlett for writing the amazing foreword for this book. It means the world to me. You taught me to really #ThinkBig

I say thank you to the amazing Sylvie di Giusto. Your are not only a fantastic speaker and image consultant, but also a great friend, who opened many doors for me. I can't express how thankful I am.

Thanks to all the members and fellow speakers of the National Speakers Association. I met so many new friends in this great organization. See you in Phoenix 2016.

Of course, I'd also like to thank my European speaker buddies. Thank you for your support, your friendship and all the deep conversations we had. You know who you are.

Thanks to my friend Oliver Kind for that legendary trip to Kramski in Pforzheim. We just did it!

A big thank you goes to you, to all my customers, readers and audiences all over the world. You're the reason I'm doing what I do.

And last, but not least, I'd like to thank my family. My parents Karin and Joachim. My sister Alexa. My grandma Friedel. Silke, the love of my life. Most of all, my two daughters, Emma and Elisabeth. Since you joined my life, nothing is as it was before. I love you all deeply!

An Offer You Can't Refuse

So you said the words: "I'm just going to do it!" You made the decision to change your business, your career or any other part of your life. My biggest intention writing this book was to help you look at the challenges of everyday life from a new perspective, to take matters in your own hands and to design your future with courage and passion. If you need any kind of support on that journey, I'm happy to help you change. As a mentor, change consultant or keynote speaker who either will pull you, push you, challenge you or inspire you, here is what I can do for you:

Keynote Speeches and Change Presentations

You are planning a company meeting, a convention or any other kind of event? Hire me as your next speaker and you can be sure that I will move your audience. I will make them think, laugh, and, most importantly, take action. That means: Lasting motivation, entertaining storytelling and lots of *Oh Yeah!* moments for your customers, employees and business partners. To hire me for your next event, please write an email to: speeches@grzeskowitz.com or visit my website: http://www.grzeskowitz.com/keynote-speaker-change/

Change Consulting

Your company needs to make a change, or is currently facing various challenges? I am a highly valued Changemaker who is famous for his hands-on approach and quick results. Whatever you need, we will find the right solution for your problem. Please write an email to: change@grzeskowitz.com or visit my website: http://www.grzeskowitz.com/change-management-consulting/

1 to 1 Coaching

Your life is changing? You want to boost your career, are searching for alternatives to your current job or want to change something else? Let me be your personal mentor and change coach on your journey. Please write an email to: coaching@grzeskowitz.com or visit my website: http://www.grzeskowitz.com/change-coaching-programs/

Bibliography

The Spotify Playlist: You can listen to that soundtrack via this Spotify-Playlist: https://open.spotify.com/user/1121732507/playlist/0zG13YabICTAbyoCGdPpcJ | Or use the Spotify App and search for "Ilja Grzeskowitz"

Branson, Richard: Richard Branson about the power of having a mission: http://www.virgin.com/richard-branson/when-you-challenge-people-they-surprise-you

Clocky, the alarm clock - Do you want to buy Clocky? Here's the link: http://www.amazon.com/Clocky-Aqua-Runaway-Alarm-Clock/dp/B000TAS9XQ

Eat Pray Love: The book is written by Elizabeth Gilbert, the movie is starring Julia Roberts in the leading role: http://www.amazon.com/Eat-Pray-Love-Julia-Roberts/dp/B00493E1GI

Gallup Study: http://www.gallup.com/services/178514/state-american-workplace.aspx

Gladwell, Malcom: Outliers – *The Story of Success*, Penguin 2009

Godin, Seth: Purple Cow: *Transform your Business by being remarkable*, Penguin 2005

Goldsmith, Marshall: *What Got You Here Won't Get You There: How Successful People Become Even More Successful*, Profile Books, 2008

Grzeskowitz, Ilja: *Die Veränderungs-Formel: Aus Problemen Chancen machen*, GABAL 2014, 2nd Printing (The change formula: Turning problems into chances)

Kotter, John P.: *Leading Change: How to change your business in 8 steps*, Vahlen 2011

Ma, Jack: The story of Jack Ma: https://en.wikipedia.org/wiki/Jack_Ma

Modern Motivation with the Pavlok Bracelet: http://www.mobiflip.de/pavlov-fitness-armband-traeger-elektroschocks/

My Facebook Page: http://www.facebook.com/igrzeskowitz

My Instagram profile www.instagram.com/igrzeskowitz

Nam June Paik: https://en.wikipedia.org/wiki/Nam_June_Paik

Mullet= Business in the front, party in the back

Pink, Daniel H.: *Drive – What really motivates you,* Ecowin, 2010

Ratelband, Emil: http://de.wikipedia.org/wiki/Emile_Ratelband

Saint Exupéry, Antoine de: The quote from *The Little Prince* goes like this: "Here is my secret. It is very simple: It is only with the heart that one can see rightly; what is essential is invisible to the eye."

Shackleton, Ernest: All about Sir Ernest Shackleton: https://en.wikipedia.org/wiki/Ernest_Shackleton

Sprenger, Reinhard: Mythos Motivation – *Wege aus einer Sackgasse,* Campus 2014 (Motivation myth – Ways out of a dead-end-street)

The Batman trilogy: http://www.amazon.com/Knight-Trilogy-Batman-Begins-Rises/dp/B009JBWOU0

The illusion of superiority: http://en.wikipedia.org/wiki/Illusory_superiority

The definition of Motivation: http://de.wikipedia.org/wiki/Motivation

The escape scene in "The Dark Knight Rises": https://www.youtube.com/watch?v=DjffIi2Pl7M

The famous bumblebee anecdote: http://www.livescience.com/33075-how-bees-fly.html

The Gaucho dance: https://www.youtube.com/watch?v=lfhCnYAVz8M

The iOS-Evolution: See: http://www.theverge.com/2011/12/13/2612736/ios-history-iphone-ipad

The legendary interview with the "ice ton": https://www.youtube.com/watch?v=m64Y6-ZpFt0

The longest list of excuses in the world: http://www.grzeskowitz.de/das-ende-der-ausreden-ein-manifest/

The mullet haircut of the 80's: https://en.wikipedia.org/wiki/Mullet_%28haircut%29

Values: https://en.wikipedia.org/wiki/Value_%28personal_and_cultural%29

GABAL global
English Editions by GABAL Publishing

Who We Are

GABAL provides proven practical knowledge and publishes media products on the topics of business, success, and life. With over 600 experienced, international authors from various industries and education, we inspire businesses and people to move forward.

GABAL. Your publisher.
Motivating. Sympathetic. Pragmatic.

These three adjectives describe the core brand of GABAL. They describe how we think, feel, and work. They describe the style and mission of our books and media. GABAL is your publisher, because we want to bring you forward. Not with finger-pointing, not divorced from reality, not pointy-headed or purely academic, but motivating in effect, sympathetic in appearance, and pragmatically-oriented toward results.

Our books have only one concern: they want to help the reader improve. In business. For success. In life.

Our target reader
People who want to develop personally and/or professionally

As a modern media house GABAL publishes books, audio books, and e-books for people and companies that want to develop further. Our books are aimed at people who are looking for knowledge about current issues in business and education that can be put into practice quickly.

For more information, see the GABAL global website:

http://www.iuniverse.com/Packages/GABAL-Global-Editions.aspx

Printed in the United States
By Bookmasters